About the Fraser Institute

The **Fraser Institute** is an independent Canadian economic and social research and educational organization. It has as its objective the redirection of public attention to the role of competitive markets in providing for the well-being of Canadians. Where markets work, the Institute's interest lies in trying to discover prospects for improvement. Where markets do not work, its interest lies in finding the reasons. Where competitive markets have been replaced by government control, the interest of the Institute lies in documenting objectively the nature of the improvement or deterioration resulting from government intervention.

The **Fraser Institute** is a national, federally-chartered, non-profit organization financed by the sale of its publications and the tax-deductible contributions of its members, foundations, and other supporters; it receives no government funding.

Editorial Advisory Board

Prof. Armen Alchian
Prof. Jean-Pierre Centi
Prof. Michael Parkin
Prof. L.B. Smith
Prof. J.M. Buchanan
Prof. Herbert G. Grubel
Prof. Friedrich Schneider
Sir Alan Walters
Prof. Edwin G. West

Senior Fellows

Murray Allen, MD
Dr. Paul Brantingham
Prof. Steve Easton
Prof. Tom Flanagan
Dr. Herbert Grubel
Prof. Rainer Knopff
Prof. Ken McKenzie
Prof. Lydia Miljan
Prof. Eugene Beaulieu
Prof. Barry Cooper
Prof. Herb Emery
Gordon Gibson
Prof. Ron Kneebone
Dr. Owen Lippert
Prof. Jean-Luc Migue
Dr. Filip Palda
Prof. Chris Sarlo

Administration

Executive Director, Michael Walker
Director, Finance and Administration, Michael Hopkins
Director, Alberta Initiative, Barry Cooper
Director, Communications, Suzanne Walters
Director, Development, Sherry Stein
Director, Education Programs, Annabel Addington
Director, Events and Conferences, Lorena Baran
Director, Publication Production, J. Kristin McCahon

Research

Director, Fiscal and Non-Profit Studies, Jason Clemens
Director, School Performance Studies, Peter Cowley
Acting Director, Pharmaceutical Policy Research, John R. Graham
Director, Centre for Studies in Risk and Regulation, Laura Jones
Director, Social Affairs Centre, Fred McMahon
Director, Education Policy, Claudia Rebanks Hepburn
Senior Research Economist, Joel Emes

Ordering publications

To order additional copies of this book, any of our other publications, or a catalogue of the Institute's publications, please contact the book sales coordinator:

    via our **toll-free order line: 1.800.665.3558, ext. 580**
    via telephone: 604.688.0221, ext. 580
    via fax: 604.688.8539
    via e-mail: sales@fraserinstitute.ca.

Media and website

For media information, please contact Suzanne Walters, Director of Communications:

    via telephone: 604.714.4582 3; or, from Toronto, 416.363.6575, ext. 582
    via e-mail: suzannew@fraserinstitute.ca

To learn more about the Institute and to read our publications on line, please visit our web site at www.fraserinstitute.ca.

Membership

For information about membership in The Fraser Institute, please contact the Development Department: The Fraser Institute, 4th Floor, 1770 Burrard Street, Vancouver, BC, V6J 3G7; or

    via telephone: 604.688.0221 ext. 586
    via fax: 604.688.8539
    via e-mail: membership@fraserinstitute.ca.

In Calgary, please contact us
    via telephone: 403.216.7175
    via fax: 403.234.9010
    via e-mail: paulineh@fraserinstitute.ca.

In Toronto, please contact us
    via telephone: 416.363.6575
    via fax: 416.601.7322.

Publication

Editing and design by Kristin McCahon and Lindsey Thomas Martin
Cover design by Brian Creswick @ GoggleBox.

International Evidence on the Effects of Having No Capital Gains Taxes

International Evidence on the Effects of Having No Capital Gains Taxes

EDITED BY HERBERT G. GRUBEL

The Fraser Institute

Vancouver   British Columbia   Canada

2001

Copyright ©2001 by The Fraser Institute. All rights reserved. No part of this book may be reproduced in any manner whatsoever without written permission except in the case of brief passages quoted in critical articles and reviews.

The authors of this book have worked independently and opinions expressed by them are, therefore, their own, and do not necessarily reflect the opinions of the members or the trustees of The Fraser Institute.

Printed in Canada.

National Library of Canada Cataloguing in Publication Data

Main entry under title:
International evidence on the effects of having no capital gains taxes

Papers from the Symposium on Capital Gains held Sept. 15, 2000 in Vancouver, BC
Includes bibliographical references.
ISBN 0-88975-189-7

1. Capital gains tax.   2. Capital gains tax--Canada.   I. Grubel, Herbert G., 1934-   II. Fraser Institute (Vancouver, B.C.)   III. Symposium on Capital Gains (2000 : Vancouver, B.C.).

HJ4631.I57 2001   336.24'24   C2001-911442-7

Table of contents

About the authors / vii

Preface / x

Acknowledgments / xiv

1   Capital gains taxes in Canada

    The case for the elimination of capital
gains taxes in Canada / 3
        Herbert G. Grubel

2   Capital gains tax regimes abroad—
countries without capital gains taxes

    Tax avoidance due to the zero capital gains tax:
Some indirect evidence from Hong Kong / 39
        Berry F.C. Hsu and Chi-Wa Yuen

    Capital gains taxation: evidence from Switzerland / 55
        Peter Kugler and Carlos Lenz

    Capital gains tax: The New Zealand case / 73
        Robin Oliver

    Capital gains taxation in Mexico and the integration
of corporation and personal taxes / 89
        Francisco Gil Diaz

3   Capital gains tax regimes abroad—
    countries with inflation indexing

   **Capital gains taxation in Britain: The merit
   of indexing and tapering**   /   107
      Barry Bracewell-Milnes

   Indexation and Australian capital gains taxation   /   123
      John Freebairn

   Capital gains taxation in Ireland   /   141
      Moore McDowell

About the authors

BARRY BRACEWELL-MILNES is an author and consultant on economic and tax policy. He has degrees from Oxford and Cambridge and was advisor to Erasmus University, Rotterdam (1973–1980) and to the Institute of Directors, London (1973–1996). He has written 25 books.

FRANCISCO GIL-DÍAZ was CEO and President of Avantel (a joint venture between Banamex, a Mexican banking group, and WorldCom). Before that, he held numerous, high-ranking executive positions in the public sector. Since early 2001, he has been the Financial Secretary (Minister of Finance) of Mexico. He holds a B.A. in Economics from ITAM, the Technological Institute of Mexico and an M.A. and a Ph.D. from the University of Chicago. He has taught Economics part-time at various institutions and, between 1970 and 1978, was Chairman of the Economics Department at ITAM. Gil-Díaz has published extensively on topics such as public finance, exchange-rate policy, macroeconomic management and deregulation of economic activity.

JOHN FREEBAIRN is a Professor and Head of the Department of Economics, University of Melbourne, Australia. He is a graduate of the University of New England and the University of California, Davis. His research interests are taxation reform, unemployment, and the pricing of infrastructure.

HERBERT GRUBEL is a Senior Fellow and holds the David Somerville Chair at The Fraser Institute. He is a Professor of Economics (Emeritus) at Simon Fraser University, where he has taught since 1971. He received a B.A. from Rutgers University, and a Ph.D. in

---

Where a chapter has more than one author, biographical information is given only for the co-author who attended the symposium in Vancouver.

economics from Yale University. He has taught full-time at Stanford University, the University of Chicago, and the University of Pennsylvania and has had temporary appointments at universities in Berlin, Singapore, Cape Town, Nairobi, Oxford, and Canberra. He was the elected Reform Party Member of Parliament for Capilano-Howe Sound from 1993 to 1997 and served as the Finance Critic from 1995 to 1997. He has published 16 books and 180 professional articles in economics dealing with international trade and finance and a wide range of economic policy issues.

PETER KUGLER has been a Professor of Economics at the University of Basel in Switzerland since 1997. Formerly, he was professor of Statistics at the University of Basel (1984–1986), Professor of Econometrics at the University of Bern (Switzerland, 1987–1993) and Professor of Economics at the University of Vienna (Austria). He has published, in refereed journals, over 50 articles on macroeconomics and (international) monetary economics as well as applied econometrics.

MOORE MCDOWELL is a Senior Lecturer in Political Economy at University College Dublin. He has degrees from University College Dublin (National University of Ireland at Dublin) and Oxford. He has been a senior Lecturer in Political Economy at University College Dublin since 1990 and has taught at San Francisco State University (1977/1978) University of California at Davis (1978, 1983, 1984/1985), and the University of Delaware (1988, 1990, 1993). His areas of teaching and research are industrial organization, public sector, and competition policy. He has written numerous papers, provided expert testimony in competition law, done advisory work in mergers, and some industry studies.

ROBIN M. OLIVER has been General Manager, Policy, Inland Revenue Department, Government of New Zealand since June 1995. In this position, he is responsible to the Commissioner of Inland Revenue for the Department's Policy Advice Division, one of the four business units into which Inland Revenue is divided. The Policy Advice Division is responsible for providing all aspects of the Department's policy advice to the Government. It also includes the international tax section, which handles the negotiation, administration, and interpretation of New Zealand's Double Tax Agreements with other countries. Prior to joining the Inland Revenue Department, Mr Oliver was a taxation partner in the international accounting firm of Arthur Andersen. A well-known adviser and commentator on taxation matters, Robin is a co-author of a text on the taxation of financial arrangements in New Zealand.

CHI-WA YUEN is an Associate Professor at the School of Economics and Finance, University of Hong Kong, Hong Kong. He obtained his Ph.D. in economics from the University of Chicago in 1991. His doctoral thesis is about the design of dynamic optimal taxation in a human-capital-based growth environment. He is the author of many articles in academic journals and a co-author in the latest edition of a popular graduate text in open economy macroeconomics, *Fiscal Policies and Growth in the World Economy* (MIT Press, 1996), originally written by Jacob Frenkel and Assaf Razin in 1987 and 1992.

Preface

International Evidence on the Effects of Having No Capital Gains Taxes represents the second part of my ongoing effort to study the costs and benefits of capital gains taxation in Canada. The first part of this effort involved a colloquium among 25 economists and entrepreneurs from Canada and the United States who met in June 1999 for the Fraser Institute 1999 Symposium on Capital Gains Taxation. We discussed the question: "Resolved that Canada's capital gains tax rate should be equal to that of the United States." Drawing on this discussion, I wrote a monograph entitled *Unlocking Canadian Capital: The Case for Capital Gains Tax Reform* (Vancouver, BC: The Fraser Institute, 2000). The main conclusion of my study was that the capital gains tax rate in Canada was too high and that lowering it would increase revenues, have little effect on the distribution of personal income, and bring large economic benefits.

During 1999 and early 2000, the Senate of Canada held a series of hearings about the merit of the capital gains tax. *Unlocking Canadian Capital* included the proceedings of five of these Senate hearings, all of which supported and expanded on the arguments I had presented in the first half of the volume. During the same period, the *Financial Post* published a number of articles by economists, including myself, who argued the case for lower capital gains tax rates in Canada.

The Liberal government in Ottawa did not respond officially to the arguments made in these studies. However, it acted as if it had been persuaded by them. It lowered the effective rate of capital gains taxation by about one-third in two distinct steps. The first, announced in the February 2000 Federal Budget, lowered the percentage of realized capital gains that had to be included in personal income tax returns from 75% to 66.66% for gains realized after February 28. The second was announced in the mini-budget leading up to the election in November 2000. It reduced the inclusion rate further to 50% for gains realized after October 17, 2000.

In effect, these policies reduced the maximum rate of personal capital gains taxation to between 23% and 25% from about 40% at the highest marginal tax rate on Canadian federal and provincial taxes combined. As a result, the Canadian rates came close to those of the United States, though comparisons are complicated. Canada applies the same rate to all gains regardless of the holding period of the assets while the United States rates for short-term gains are higher than those for long-term gains.

The first of the rate reductions was welcomed immediately by the investment community in Canada. The criticism normally expected from the political left did not materialize. The positive public reaction to the first cut undoubtedly encouraged the government to make the further reductions later in the year. It is somewhat surprising that these policies also failed to elicit any negative response from the political left or the general public.

It is not clear why Canadians were so ready to accept these lower capital gains tax rates passed in 2000. It is possible that the cuts were acceptable because they were part of a broader range of tax reductions made while the fiscal surplus was high and forecast to grow rapidly. A further cause for the lack of public protest may have been the fact that the cuts merely reduced the capital gains tax rates to the level that had prevailed until the 1994 Budget. These rates presumably had been arrived at after much debate and consultation and had become accepted as a necessary part of a fair and efficient tax system.

In addition, it is almost certain that the barrage of studies of the harmful effects of capital gains taxation noted above has played an important role in the government's decision to lower rates. In my view, most of the arguments presented in these publications made a persuasive case not only for lower rates of capital gains taxation but for the complete elimination of the tax. Almost everyone present at the symposium agreed that such a policy would increase the rate of capital formation, foreign investment, and growth in productivity and, therefore, raise the living standards of all Canadians. However, these benefits are seen by many to bring some important costs in terms of lower overall government revenue, requiring higher taxes on other forms of income. The elimination of the capital gains tax is also considered to make the income distribution less equal and, most important, cause strong incentives for tax avoidance.

The question for public policy therefore is: Do the benefits from the elimination of the tax in terms of higher income outweigh the costs of lower revenues, greater inequality of income, and incentives for tax avoidance? Unfortunately, the answer to this question must be based to a large extent on judgements rather than solid empirical evidence, in part because the history of capital gains taxation in Canada is too short and involves too few changes in rates and coverage to allow the kinds of econometric studies needed to measure the important changes objectively.

This state of affairs did not prevent the Senate Committee Report to reach the following conclusion, after it had listened to a number of expert witnesses:

> For all of the above reasons, the Committee believes that a further, substantial reduction in the capital gains tax rate is warranted. Indeed, as markets for goods and services become increasingly globalized, and because international competition for capital rests ultimately on after tax rates of return, Canada cannot ignore developments elsewhere in the world. Therefore, at a minimum, we recommend that the Canadian capital gains tax rate should quickly be lowered to match the rate in the United States. However, this is probably insufficient. A tax rate even lower than the American rate is more appropriate, as other nations have concluded ... Thus, the Committee also recommends that international competitiveness be the criterion guiding the choice of a capital gains tax regime, and that the federal government be prepared to lower the tax until that criterion is met. (*Senate Banking Committee Report on Capital Gains Taxation* 2000: 22)

Table 1 provides information about the capital gains tax regime of major foreign countries. This information is not easy to obtain and has been compiled by Arthur Andersen through a special survey and from information from Deloite Touche and KPMG. The table has been adapted by me by drawing on Appendix A of the *Senate Banking Committee Report on Capital Gains Taxation* (2000).

This table not only is important in understanding the need for Canada to consider international competitiveness in setting policy on capital gains taxation. It also shows that there are a number of

Table 1: Capital gains tax provisions in selected countries (rates on individuals, maximum rates on gains from equities)

	Short-term	Long-term	Holding period
Argentina	Exempt	Exempt	No
Australia	24.5	24.5; inflation indexing	No
Belgium	Exempt	Exempt	No
Brazil	15.0	15.0	No
Canada	23–25	23–25	No
Chile	45.0; exclusion $6,600/yr	45.0; exclusion $6,600/yr	No
China	20.0; specific shares	20.0; specific shares	No
Denmark	40.0	40.0; some exemptions	3 years
France	26.0; exclusion $8,315/yr	26.0; exclusion $8,315/yr	No
Germany	55.9	Exempt	6 month
Hong Kong	Exempt	Exempt	No
India	30.0	20.0	1 year
Indonesia	0.1	0.1	No
Ireland	20.0	20.0	No
Italy	12.5	12.5	No
Japan	1.25% of sales price or 20% of net gain	1.25% of sales price or 20% of net gain	No
Korea	20.0; share traded on major exchange exempt	20.0; share traded on major exchange exempt	No
Mexico	Exempt	Exempt	No
Netherlands	Exempt	Exempt	No
Poland	Exempt	Exempt	No
Singapore	Exempt	Exempt	No
Sweden	30.0	30.0	No
Taiwan	Exempt	Exempt	No
United Kingdom	40.0; some exemptions	10.0 to 40%; Rate dependent on holding period	Sliding scale
United States	39.6	20.0	1 year

Source: Adapted from Senate Banking Committee (2000), Appendix A. See source for more details and source of data.

countries in the world that have considerable experience in running a tax system without capital gains taxation. Because this experience is useful in shedding light on the likely consequences of adopting a capital gains tax rate of zero in Canada, in September 2000 The Fraser Institute held the 2000 Symposium on Capital Gains Taxation (September 15, 2000) at which economists from nine countries addressed a number of issues that I consider important in assessing the consequences of having no capital gains tax. Some of the papers discussed countries' experiences with the use of indexing of capital gains due to inflation.

Part 1 of the present study presents my views on the merit of eliminating Canada's capital gains tax and is based on the existing, traditional literature. It also summarizes the main findings of the papers presented at the gathering. Part 2 contains seven papers written by the participants at the symposium.

Herbert G. Grubel

Acknowledgments

The 2000 Symposium was made possible by the generous support of the John Dobson Foundation of Montreal. At The Fraser Institute, Lorena Baran and Adele Waters provided outstanding logistic support for those attending. Kristin McCahon and Lindsey Thomas Martin were responsible for the production of this conference volume. Joel Emes provided me with excellent notes of the discussions. Besides the authors of the papers included in this volume, the following participants contributed valuable insights during the symposium: Jason Clemens, The Fraser Institute; Professor Sijbren Cnossen, Erasmus University; John Dobson, Dobson Foundation, Montreal; Professor Steve Easton, Simon Fraser University; Professor Jonathan Kesselman, University of British Columbia; Alan Reynolds, The Hudson Institute; Munir Sheikh, Department of Finance, Ottawa; Professor Ruul van den Dool, Erasmus University; David Somerville, Calgary; Professor Zane Spindler, Simon Fraser University; Michael Walker, The Fraser Institute; and Professor Thomas Wilson, University of Toronto.

1 Capital gains taxes in Canada

The case for the elimination of capital gains taxes in Canada

HERBERT G. GRUBEL

Introduction

In this part of *International Evidence on the Effects of Having No Capital Gains Taxes,* I present theoretical arguments about the economic benefits and costs that may be expected to arise from the elimination of the capital gains tax in Canada. I also consider the effects of such a policy on the distribution of income and on the incentives by taxpayers to shift taxable income into non-taxable capital gains.

Throughout the chapter, I refer to material contained in the papers printed in Parts 2 and 3 of this volume and presented at the 2000 Fraser Institute Symposium on Capital Gains. My chapter concludes with the case for, and the case against, the full indexation of capital gains. In doing so, I summarize the main findings from some of the papers found in Part 2.

Optimal tax theory and capital taxes

The economic theory of optimal taxation was developed during the last 25 years and the Oxford economist James Mirrlees received a Nobel Prize for his contributions to this body of knowledge. This theory argues that the economic cost of taxation is higher the more easily the tax can be avoided by those required to pay it. By these standards, the capital gains tax is the worst tax of all. Taxpayers can avoid paying it simply by not realizing their capital gains. They can reduce their level of savings and invest in assets with low probabilities of generating capital gains. Foreigners, especially Americans, keep their assets at home or come to Canada only if the pre-tax returns make up for the taxes they have to pay.

All of these tax-induced changes reduce the rate at which gains in labour productivity—and, therefore, living standards—is increased. Capital that is "locked in" earns lower economic returns. Less investment by Canadians and foreigners reduces labour productivity directly and slows the introduction of new technology embodied in capital. Less investment is made in high-risk projects and the engine of innovation and growth is starved.

The Canadian Department of Finance has published estimates of the losses in output resulting from an extra dollar of tax. Unfortunately, the estimates do not include the capital gains tax but the corporate income tax may stand as a proxy for the capital gains tax since both fall on the capital and create very similar incentives and opportunities to avoid them. The estimates, published by the OECD (1997), suggest that an extra dollar raised by the corporate income tax costs $1.55 in output. The analogous figures are $.56 for the personal income tax, $.27 for the payroll tax and only $.17 for the sales tax. These data suggest strongly that the elimination of the capital gains tax and a simultaneous increase in other taxes to maintain total revenue would cause national income to increase—and lead to overall higher tax revenues as people with higher incomes paid more taxes.

How big is the effect on output?

It is very difficult, however, to make reliable, reproducible, quantitative estimates of the direct effects of capital gains taxation on productivity and living standards. In Canada and other economies there are too many other influences operating on productivity and output. These confounding influences are a function, for example, of the level and structure of the personal and corporate income taxes, the effects of terms of trade, environmental legislation and other regulations, labour market flexibility, inflation, interest rates, and shocks like the energy crisis. There are not enough observations and too few changes in the rate of taxation, and the interrelationships are too complex to permit separating out the effects of high capital gains taxes on economic growth in Canada.

However, there are two ways, less rigorous but still useful, to shed light on the empirical effects of capital gains taxes on economic performance. The first involves the judgement of persons who have access to input from a wide range of practitioners. The following quotations are from two distinguished persons in this position.

> The tax on capital gains directly affects investment decisions, the mobility and flow of risk capital ... the ease or difficulty experienced by new ventures in obtaining capital, and therefore the strength and potential for growth in the economy.
> *President John F. Kennedy, Special Message to the Congress on Tax Reduction and Reform, January 24, 1963 (quoted in Joint Economic Committee 1999)*

> The point I made at the Budget Committee was that if the capital gains tax were eliminated, that we would presumably, over time, see increased economic growth ... Indeed, its major impact is to impede entrepreneurial activity and capital formation. While all taxes impede economic growth to one extent or another, the capital gains tax is at the far end of the scale. I argued that the appropriate capital gains tax rate was zero.
> *Federal Reserve Chairman Alan Greenspan in testimony before the Senate Banking Committee on February 25, 1997 (quoted in Joint Economic Committee 1999)*

The second method for obtaining information about the effect of capital gains taxation on economic growth is to consider the experience of countries with different capital gains tax regimes. Simple and imperfect as the evidence might be, it is interesting to note that according to my own calculations (Grubel 2000: 39), five countries without capital gains taxes (Hong Kong, the Netherlands, New Zealand, Singapore and Switzerland) during the years 1990 to 1997 had average annual rates of growth in real per-capita income equal to 2.2%. The remaining member countries of the OECD grew at only 1.2% annually during the same period.

Objections to abolishing the capital gains tax

If we accept the evidence that the abolition of the capital gains tax will increase economic growth in Canada, what are the objections to this policy? I discussed these objections in *Unlocking Canadian Capital*. Below is a summary of my findings, supplemented by new information obtained through the recent symposium and the papers in this volume.

What effect on revenue?

The first justification for capital gains taxes is that they are needed to raise revenue and thus permit lower taxes on personal and business income and sales (the GST). This justification is valid only in a static view of the world. In fact, in most countries, lower capital gains taxes have increased the realization of capital gains and thus resulted in higher revenues. The evidence on this process is very strong for the short run but many analysts insist that it also works in the longer run because of the effect of lower capital gains taxes on economic growth.

The higher growth rates of countries without capital gains taxes discussed above imply that if Canada abandons the tax, revenues from other taxes will eventually increase enough to compensate for the lost revenues. According to our estimates explained in table 1 of Grubel (2000), the 1992 capital gains tax revenues were only $716 million or 0.3% of all Canadian government revenues of $277.5 billion. Therefore, if the elimination of the capital gains tax raises the *level* of income and, therefore, the tax base by a mere 0.3%, the losses will be wiped out and remain at zero into the indefinite future. If the rate of growth is raised, the losses will also be eliminated and surpluses will arise thereafter.

How likely is it that the elimination of the capital gains tax will bring such benefits? The data on OECD countries with and without taxes has already been presented above in support of the notion that growth will increase. However, the relevance of these data for Canada might be questioned because of the special characteristics of the countries without the tax. Hong Kong and Singapore are regarded increasingly as countries with such unique conditions that their experience is irrelevant for the industrial countries of the West. The success of the Netherlands is based on policies that would be considered unacceptable in Canada and may well have brought only short-lived benefits.

Evidence from Switzerland by Kugler and Lenz

It is important, therefore, that the chapter by Peter Kugler and Carlos Lenz (p. 55) presents unique, powerful empirical evidence on the effect the elimination of the capital gains tax has had on income in Switzerland. According to the authors, the federal government of Switzerland does not impose a capital gains tax. However, most cantons in that country have had such taxes for some time but, in recent years, some of these cantons have eliminated the capital gains tax and others retained it. These conditions supply us with a rare opportunity in the social sciences, the equivalent of a controlled experiment. One sample of countries changes one policy while the control group of countries does not, all while other policies and external conditions affecting economic conditions in the country as a whole remain unchanged.

Kugler and Lenz calculated the trend in the economic growth rates of all cantons before and after the elimination of the capital gains tax. They then calculated average growth rates for two groups of cantons, one in which capital gains taxes remained unchanged and one in which they were eliminated. They found that the cantons that eliminated the capital gains tax enjoyed an average short-run 2.2% jump in the *level* of national income relative to the other group of cantons. In the longer run, the jump in income is 3.1%.

It is possible that the cantons increased their incomes simply as a result of drawing capital and labour from cantons that had retained the capital gains tax. If this is true, the higher output in the gaining countries is matched by lower output in the losing countries and overall Switzerland is no better off. Moreover, if the argument is true, the process involves the inefficient relocation of the resources and, therefore, an actual reduction in output of all cantons. The authors examined their data for evidence on such shifting of capital and labour and found none.

What about the effect of the removal of the capital gains tax on economic growth rates rather than levels? The authors note that the time series available to them is too short to estimate such an effect.

In spite of the limitations of the study of the Swiss experience, the results are consistent with so-called "supply-side economics" and its hallmark "Laffer curve." According to this theory, it is not surprising that the recent tax cuts of Ireland, the United States and the continued low taxes in Hong Kong and Singapore resulted in more rapid economic growth than that experienced in countries with higher levels of taxation. The incentives to working, investment, risk-taking and innovation activated by lower taxes are almost certain to bring higher economic growth.

I believe that the available evidence makes a good case for the elimination of the capital gains tax in Canada. However, many economists and politicians argue against this policy because it is seen to have socially adverse effects on the distribution of income and it results in tax avoidance maneuvers as taxpayers attempt to shift taxable income into non-taxable capital gains.

What effect on income distribution?

The argument in favor of a capital gains tax has two aspects. First, it suggests that increases in the value of assets upon realization provide their owners with resources that can be used, just like higher salaries, interest, or dividend incomes, to raise consumption expenditures. Horizontal equity in taxation requires that all increases in spending power be taxed equally, regardless of their origin. This reasoning underlay the recommendation by the Carter Commission in the 1960s that a capital gains tax be imposed, using the catchy slogan "a buck is a buck." The Commission's report in turn drew on the academic analysis of Simons (1938) and Haig (1921), which made a theoretical case for a comprehensive definition of the taxable income base, which included capital gains.

The second argument in support of the capital gains tax rests on the principle of the "ability to pay." This seductive slogan is the rallying cry of the political left, which considers it self-evident that persons earning $100,000 a year can afford to pay a higher proportion of their income than those earning only $20,000. The argument from the "ability to pay" has resulted in the progressive income tax system in Canada. It forces high-income earners to pay more than 50% on marginal increases in income while those at the bottom of the scale pay no taxes at all or rates on extra income of only about 20%.

It is widely believed that only high-income earners make substantial capital gains on the grounds that lower income earners do not have savings to accumulate wealth and enjoy the capital gains it can bring. For these reasons, the capital gains tax is believed to fall mainly on high-income earners able to pay it.

What arguments can be made in response to these justifications of a capital gains tax? First, the "buck is a buck" slogan is seen faulty by many because it does not distinguish an essential feature of capital gains that make them different from ordinary income. The following slogan makes this point succinctly: "tax the fruit of the tree but not the tree itself." The idea that captial gains are different from income in this sense and, therefore, should not be taxed long dominated the tax policies of the United Kingdom and countries of its former empire like Australia, New Zealand, and Canada. The idea lost its grip only after the end of the second World War, when governments everywhere took on a much larger role in society. It was also used for a long time to fight against the imposition of a capital gains tax in the United States.

The economic analysis underlying this notion of "fruit and tree" is that taxation should fall only on sources of income that are not part of society's future productive capital essential to the maintenance of living standard. Under this principle, it is all right to tax profits, interest, and dividends but not the financial and real capital that give rise to this income. In a world without inflation, all capital gains by definition are equal to increases in the present value of the future income stream flowing from the asset. Therefore, a capital gains tax reduces an economy's productive capacity and the future stream of income.

In the presence of inflation, some capital gains simply reflect the higher cost of reproducing the capital. The taxation of such nominal capital gains reduces the country's productive capacity even more severely than does the taxation of real capital gains. In addition, the taxation of such phantom capital gains is unfair since such a punitive confiscation of real property is inconsistent with the principles of horizontal equity and ability to pay.

The "fruit-and-tree" analogy and the fact that capital gains taxation reduces the stock of productive capital provides another explanation of empirical phenomenon, noted above, that countries without capital gains have larger capital stocks and correspondingly higher labour productivity and incomes.

Canadian politicians embraced the "buck-is-a-buck" slogan very happily when it first was developed in the Carter Commission

Report in the late 1960s. It allowed them to defend their support for the tax by appealing to an easily understood and populist idea. Public-choice theory explains why demands for such a tax bring large electoral support. The number of voters with incomes below average and without capital gains in the 1960s was much greater than the number of voters with high incomes and potential capital gains. In effect, the politicians offered voters with lower incomes a transfer of income at the expense of the "rich." The electoral success of the advocates of the tax led to its adoption in 1971. The same reasons that made the tax attractive to politicians in the first place prevent its elimination now. The conventional wisdom suggests that the number of voters with low incomes and no capital gains is much greater than that of voters with high incomes and capital gains. Therefore, no political party can expect to win with a policy proposal that violates the interest of the largest segment of the population.

How correct is this conventional wisdom? Simple statistics support it. Canadians with incomes of more than $100 thousand in 1992 represented 7.9% of all taxpayers. They paid 77.9% of all capital gains taxes. The remaining 92.1% of voters paid few or no capital gains taxes.

However, this figure and the conventional wisdom are incorrect for two reasons. First, the ownership of mutual funds has spread enormously in recent decades, especially among those with modest incomes. Canadian tax laws require that capital gains made as a result of the operation of mutual funds have to be reported and are subject to taxation in the owners' annual income-tax return. This tax burden tends to come as a complete surprise to most new owners of mutual funds. (It should be noted that the tax is not payable on mutual funds held in tax-exempt Registered Retirement Savings Plans). It is clear that the tax on the realized gains falls to a considerable degree not on the rich but on Canadians with modest and even low incomes, who in recent years have increasingly become the owners of mutual funds both in, and outside, their tax-sheltered retirement plans.

Second, income earners in the highest income bracket often have such high taxable income because in the particular year they realized large capital gains. Their other, normal income before and after the year in which they realized their gains often put them into the middle-income and even lower-income brackets. Here is how this happens. Consider a person with a modest income, who has accumulated some shares and real estate to provide an income upon retirement. When such a person dies, the capital gains are deemed realized and the tax is due. Another example involves a person who owns a small business, like a restaurant or a garage. Upon retirement, the business is sold. After much hard work and plowing profits back into the business over a long time, the sale gives rise to a substantial taxable capital gain and tax obligation. Yet the often-modest income of the owners of such small businesses hardly qualifies them as "rich."

Capital gains arising from circumstances like these certainly are not in the conventional wisdom, which has it that capital gains taxes are paid by the very rich. The analysis in the preceding paragraph suggests that the elimination of the capital gains tax would not allow the "rich to get richer." Instead, it would permit many Canadians with moderate incomes to enjoy a higher living standard in their old age.

How important is the challenge to the conventional wisdom implicit in the above examples? Joel Emes at The Fraser Institute quantified the phenomenon, using statistics supplied by Revenue Canada for 1992 (SPSD/M 6.1). He subtracted capital gains from taxpayers' reported incomes and then classified these taxpayers according to the size of their remaining other income. He found that Canadians with such other income above $100,000 paid only 26.8% of all capital gains taxes. People with other incomes below $50,000 paid 52.1% of the total.

In sum, the equity arguments in favour of capital gains taxation—"a buck is a buck" and "ability to pay"—are politically appealing and explain why Canada enacted a capital gains tax. However, this appeal is reduced substantially by the little-known fact that the bulk of capital gains taxes is paid by people who have modest incomes and hold mutual fund shares. More important, many taxpayers have modest incomes in years other than the one in which they enjoy large capital gains. In addition, for anyone concerned about the absolute living standards of the low-income earners, "taxing the tree as well as the fruit" in the longer run reduces the living standards of the very people the tax is supposed to help.

I believe that for these reasons, the traditional equity argument in favour of retaining the tax has lost much of its validity and political appeal in recent years as Canadians in increasing numbers have become capitalist holders of financial assets directly or through their pension funds. The political appeal has also declined along with the much-diminished rhetoric about social classes of workers and capitalists that occurred with the end of the Communist empires. Politicians might well be surprised to find strong electoral support for the removal of the tax, especially if they explain effectively the basic facts about who pays the tax and what effects it has on income in the longer run. The absence of public objections to the lowering of the tax in 2000 supports this conclusion.

What is the incidence of the tax?

Ideologues concerned about the distribution of income between capital and labour—one of the central concerns of Karl Marx—consider the capital gains tax to be beneficial because it reduces the income of capitalists and increases that of workers. According to Marx, such a redistribution of income is considered to be essential for economic prosperity since it raises spending on consumption by workers and reduces the savings of capitalists. These results prevent the regular crises of unemployment brought on by overall under-consumption and too much saving. It also prevents imperialism and the opportunity it brings for industrial countries to unload surplus production on developing countries and thus prevent over-production and unemployment—while destroying the indigenous industries of these countries.

The idea that capitalism is prone to unemployment crises due to too little spending has been made respectable by Keynesian economics and still dominates the thinking of the political left in Canada. It is used to argue in favour of higher taxes on the rich and capitalists and more government spending to raise the income of the lower-income classes and workers.

At the first (1999) Fraser Institute symposium on capital gains taxation, Professor John Chant pointed to a puzzling phenomenon in the theory of tax incidence. Public-finance textbooks make much out of the proposition that tax burdens often are shifted away from producers and sellers of products and in the end are borne by consumers. For example, a tax on the sale of wood products may appear to lead to lower incomes for their producers. In fact, almost all of the cost of the tax is passed on to consumers through higher prices of the goods.

Chant pointed out that these same books do not apply an equivalent analysis of the incidence of the capital gains tax. Yet, if they did, it would be obvious that the traditional incidence model produces clear and simple results for a small country. Since Canada is a small country and capital is imported freely, the rate of return on capital is set abroad. Now, if the government of Canada imposes any tax on the holders of capital—including a capital gains tax—returns in Canada are lowered below the world level. Foreigners refuse to accept the lower rate and Canadians shift more of their capital abroad. As a result, the stock of capital in Canada is lowered and pre-tax rates of return increase correspondingly until post-tax rates of return reach those prevailing in the rest of the world.

In this new equilibrium, the capital per worker in Canada is lower than it was before the tax was imposed. The lower capital endowment reduces the productivity and, therefore, the income of workers. Through this process, the tax on capital ends up being borne by workers, which is not at all the effect desired by the ideologues mentioned above who want the capitalists' share of income to be reduced to assure higher spending on consumption. And, it certainly is not the effect desired by those who are concerned about the absolute standards of living of workers at all levels of income.

Professor Zane Spindler, who participated in both Fraser Institute symposiums on capital taxation, recently has entered the debate over the institution of a capital gains tax in South Africa (Spindler 2001). He uses a model based on the incidence analysis just presented to show how a capital gains reduces the stock of domestic capital. He then goes on to argue that this lower capital stock has two additional negative effects on welfare not accounted for by the lower labour productivity associated with the smaller stock of capital per worker.

The rigorous analysis of these additional costs is too technical to be presented here. Suffice it to note that one of these effects is what economists call the deadweight loss caused by the government tax. Deadweight loss tends to be relatively small because it reflects essentially the lost opportunity of individuals to trade freely. A Canadian who would have borrowed capital at 8% in New York in the absence of a capital gains tax, is forced to pay 10% to a domestic lender. At this interest cost, the project might not be undertaken at all. The Canadian turns his or her labour to other investment projects that, by definition, are inferior to that prevented by the existence of the capital gains tax.

The second negative effect of the capital gains tax is that it gives rise to government revenue, which is matched by costs to the taxpayers. As Professor Gordon Tullock (1967) has pointed out, these taxes invite payers to lobby with politicians and bureaucrats to exempt them from the payment. This activity by taxpayers is called "rent seeking" and uses up real resources in the form of labour and other resources spent on persuading the bureaucrats and politicians to provide the special concessions. The invitations to fancy entertainment and travel, the offer of lucrative positions in the private sector, and so on are well known in principle but difficult to observe directly. However, Tullock argues persuasively that as long as there are taxes payable, it pays to lobby to be exempted. The process ends only once all of the potential tax revenue is matched by the costs of lobbying.

It may well be that the theoretical Tullock model overestimates the real resource costs of lobbying for exemption from government taxes and regulations. But, as a former elected member of the Parliament of Canada, I can testify to the fact that anyone in such a position can be entertained over dinner virtually every day of the week. My experience as a member of an opposition party surely is only indicative of the costly lobbying that goes on with members of Parliament who serve in cabinet and have real power to influence the bureaucratic administration of laws and regulations.

Finally, it is worth noting that in the preceding analysis it was assumed implicitly that the real investment undertaken by foreigners or financed by Canadians with borrowed funds only yields returns reflected in profits and dividends. This is not true, according to the modern theories of economic growth and trade (Porter et al. 1988) and Romer 1986). Direct foreign investment brings knowledge and training to domestic workers that they can use in other employment. Some former workers of multinational businesses use their knowledge and skills to form companies that compete with their former employers, fill the need for specific inputs used by the foreign company, or offer specialized marketing services. These new activities of former employees of foreign direct investment raise overall productivity in Canada in ways that are not attributed to the initial foreign investment. These so-called externalities are lost to the extent that a capital gains tax reduces the magnitude of direct foreign investment.

Another form of externality arises from the cluster of industries in related activities (Porter 1980). Outstanding examples of such clusters are the centers for high-tech firms in the Silicon Valley in California and the Ottawa Valley in Ontario. In these areas, the technical, financial, marketing, and other experts of individual firms meet regularly in formal or informal gatherings. Valuable information, the driving force of modern industry, is exchanged in, often subtle, ways and raises the productivity of all firms in the areas. Direct foreign investment, especially by multinationals, contributes to these externalities, often by contributing knowledge gathered at other clusters around the world. These externalities raise productivity and incomes in Canada. They are lost to the extent that capital gains taxation reduces the inflow of direct foreign investment.

What are the administrative and efficiency costs?

One of the most important objections to the removal of the capital gains tax is that it would create powerful incentives for taxpayers to shift taxable income into non-taxable capital gains. Such practices cause the misallocation of resources and greater income inequalities since people with lower incomes would not have opportunities to reduce their overall tax burden.

Many economists consider the argument over the shifting of taxes very important. The practice allegedly was widespread in the years before the creation of the capital gains tax and the Department of Revenue in Canada had to spend large amounts of resources to stem the practice. A review of capital gains taxation by the Department of Finance (1980) summarized the issues in the following quotation, which is italicized in the original publication: "The inability of the government to check surplus stripping abuses was, in fact, the primary impetus for the comprehensive review of the tax system in the early 1960s. It led to the establishment of the Royal Commission on Taxation."

Some leading investors and fund managers working in the Canadian capital market during the 1950s and 1960s have told me that the problem of surplus stripping was quantitatively relatively minor. They believe that the creation of the Royal Commission and its recommendation for the creation of a capital gains tax was symbolic of a swing towards larger government and the need for higher revenues to finance it. The alleged economic success of Communism in the Soviet Union and Cuba and of Social Democracy in Sweden had created an intellectual and political environment in all industrial countries, including Canada, for the expansion of government and higher taxes.

The present opposition to the elimination of the capital gains tax in Canada focuses strongly on the problems raised by surplus stripping. It is important, therefore, to understand the concept fully. For this purpose I present the following theoretical illustration of how such "surplus stripping" would operate. It was given to the economists at the Fraser Institute symposium in the hope that they would be able to report the extent to which the practice is used in the countries that do not have a capital gains tax and how local revenue authorities have coped with it.

Surplus stripping

Table 1 illustrates how surplus stripping would work. In all parts of the table it is assumed that there is no tax on capital gains and that the marginal rate of taxation on personal income is 50%. The business tax is assumed to be 25%. (For the sake of simplicity the analysis disregards the fact that Canada uses a complicated system to reduce the double taxation of business income.)

The first part of the table shows the amount of taxes payable if earnings of the business are distributed and enter into the owner's personal income tax return. The second part shows what happens if the dividend is not paid out but reinvested. I then describe the legal maneuvers involved in stripping the reinvested dividends as tax-free capital gains.

The illustration in table 1 demonstrates clearly the incentives to reduce taxes by otherwise legal maneuvers in a tax regime that taxes personal income from assets but does not tax capital gains on such assets. The illustration also suggests that the incentives are an increasing function of the rate of taxation on personal income and a decreasing function of the tax rate on business profits, facts that help to explain Hong Kong's benign experience with zero capital gains taxes described in chapter below by Hsu and Yuen (p. 39).

Table 1 : Surplus stripping—the avoidance of personal income taxes in the absence of a capital gains tax

    (1) Pre-tax income of Company A $100.00

    (2) Less corporate income tax at 25% $25.00

    (3) Equals corporate surplus available for distribution to owner $75.00

(I) **Withdrawal of corporate surplus as dividends**

    (4) Dividend received by shareholder $75.00

    (5) Less personal income tax at 50%   37.50

    (6) Total corporate and personal income taxes (lines 3 + 5) paid by Smith, the owner of the business $62.50

(II) **Withdrawal of corporate surplus as capital gains (with capital gains tax rate at zero)—stylized facts.**

    (1) In line 3 above, it is assumed that $75 of after-tax business income is distributed to Smith. The tax evasion strategy requires that this sum is reinvested in Company A, which then shows in its balance sheet X in real assets and $75 in cash.

    (2) Smith incorporates a new Company B, which borrows a sum of money from a bank. The cash is used to buy all shares of Company A. The price of the shares does not matter. Company B now is the sole owner of all of A's real assets plus $75.

    (3) Company A uses the cash it has obtained through the previous transactions to repurchase its shares held by Company B. But B returns to A only the real assets keeps the $75 in cash.

    (4) Company A has the same balance sheet as before the reinvestment of the $75. The value of its shares matches that of its real assets.

    (5) However, Company B in the end has all the cash borrowed from the bank plus the $75 in cash. B repays the bank loan and keeps the $75 residual. This sum is a capital gain, which arose from the perfectly legal purchase and sale of the shares of A. It is paid to the owner in cash. Company B is dissolved or kept as a legal shell.

    (6) The owner reports this capital gain in his personal income tax return, but owes no tax.

    (7) Total tax paid on $100 corporate income and under the surplus stripping policy: $25.00

    Conclusion: Taxes avoided by reinvestment of profits and accompanying legal maneuvers: **$37.50**

Converting personal income into capital gains

The absence of a capital gains tax also creates incentives to convert ordinary taxable income normally paid as a salary into non-taxable income. The opportunity to avoid taxes through this process tends to be open to professionals like physicians, lawyers, and accountants and to plumbers, carpenters, and other skilled craftsmen who conduct their affairs through a wholly owned and controlled corporation. Table 2 illustrates how under these assumptions tax burdens can be reduced.

Again, it should be noted that the amount of savings from the evasion strategy is an increasing function of the personal income tax rate. It is also less the higher the rate of business taxation.

Evaluation

The preceding analysis makes it clear that the elimination of the capital gains tax in principle opens perfectly legal opportunities for the evasion of taxes, which has important implications for the overall fairness of the taxation system. However, in practice, the use of the method is limited by two factors.

First, as the description of the process shows, tax evasion through these methods is complicated and costly for small and wholly owned businesses. Second, widely held and publicly traded firms face accounting rules and market discipline, which make it virtually impossible to engage in such maneuvers.

As John Dobson, a successful Canadian portfolio manager pointed out during the symposium, the real world importance of surplus stripping and income shifting as an argument against the elimination of the capital gains tax in Canada cannot be settled by reference to the theoretical analysis alone. Needed is empirical information about the phenomenon.

As was noted above in the context of the effects of the capital gains tax on productivity, answers to complex empirical questions for which sophisticated studies cannot be made can be sought through two methods. The first involves the judgement of practical people working in the field of investment. Thus, the following quotation taken from Jude Wanniski:

Table 2: Income Shifting: The Avoidance of Personal Income Taxes in the Absence of Capital Gains Taxes.

Assume that Smith owns an incorporated business A, which receives all of his professional income and which pays all expenses. To simplify the illustration, assume that after the payment of $100 as a salary to Smith, the company has no profits.

(I) No Tax Avoidance

(1) The corporation pays Smith a salary of $100.

(2) Smith faces a marginal tax rate of 50% and therefore pays taxes of $50.

(II) Tax is Avoided

(3) The corporation A does not pay Smith a salary and, therefore, shows a profit of $100. It pays a corporate income tax of $25, leaving the business with all of its assets and liabilities plus $75 in cash.

(4) Smith now goes through the same legal maneuvers of creating Company B, taking out a cash loan, buying and selling Company B and so on described in Table 1. After the maneuver is completed, Company B is left with a capital gain of $75, which goes to the professional as a non-taxable capital gain.

(5) Total taxes paid under strategy II: $25

Conclusion: Income shifting results in tax savings of $25.

Alan Greenspan has labored in the Wall Street vineyards before he got his academic degrees in economics. He told me he had spent decades trying to figure out how to convert ordinary income to capital gains, and couldn't figure out how to do it. As he put it in a conversation in his office at the Fed, perhaps a decade ago, any tax on capital gains is a tax on the national standard of living. (Wanniski 1999)

The second approach to the gathering of empirical information is to study history and the experience of foreign jurisdictions. As the papers in this volume show, the shifting of ordinary income into non-taxable capital gains can readily be prevented by appropriate legislation. The following are the main findings of economists who studied their countries' experience with a zero capital gains tax regime.

What is the evidence from abroad?
Countries without capital gains taxes.

All of the papers printed below convey an important message. In practice, the tax systems of all countries are extremely complex and are in constant flux. Readers should be warned that for this reason alone, the summaries to be presented by their very nature involve much simplification and cannot tell the full story.

Hong Kong

The chapter on Hong Kong by Berry F. C. Hsu and Chi-Wa Yuen, *Tax Avoidance Due to the Zero Capital Gains Tax: Some Indirect Evidence from Hong Kong* (p. 39), is perhaps the most definitive in documenting that a zero capital gains tax does not bring major distortions and problems for the tax authorities. In that special administrative region of China, the battlefront between tax collectors and those wanting to reduce their tax burden is found in the operational definition of gains from trading and capital gains. The following excerpts from their paper make the main points:

> Problems arise when assets are traded as a matter of routine business, as in the case of a real estate firm specialising in the purchase and resale of buildings and land. Profits from such trade in assets are taxable. In principle, profits from the increase in the value of such property held as trading inventory are not taxable. In practical law, however, the concept of "trade" has not been precisely defined in the Inland Revenue Ordinance. As a result, courts are often asked to adjudicate disputes between citizens who claim that income is from capital gains rather than from trade and the tax authorities who argue that the income is due to trading.

> Believing in the basic principle of simplicity, the Inland Revenue Ordinance from the outset has been designed to contain very little strict anti-avoidance legislation. However, over time, the growth of sophisticated tax planning arrangements has led to the introduction of many sub-sections in the Inland Revenue Ordinance aimed at closing loopholes. Now the Inland Revenue Ordinance contains two general anti-avoidance

provisions. The first sets out to disregard any 'artificial or fictitious' transactions that do not in fact take place and any that reduce or would reduce the amount of tax payable. The second applies a 'sole or dominant purpose' test to determine whether a transaction is conducted mainly for the purpose of obtaining tax benefits through the avoidance or postponement of the liability to pay tax or the reduction in the amount thereof.

In fact, the court decisions...have not prevented attempts to avoid taxes through transactions that turn income into non-taxable capital gains. This is at least in part due to the fact that it is not always clear whether a given transaction is designed to avoid taxes or whether it is a genuine commercial activity that only appeared to involve tax evasion. As a result, a number of rulings by the Commissioner of Inland Revenue that specific transactions are for tax avoidance have been appealed to the Board of Review of the Hong Kong Inland Revenue. These appeals may be considered to reflect the extent to which the absence of a capital gains tax has induced shifting of ordinary income into capital gains.

After a review of the nature and magnitude of these appeals, the authors come to the following overall conclusion:

> On the basis of the indirect evidence available to us we conclude that the absence of a capital gains tax in Hong Kong has resulted in little, if any, inefficiencies and inequities.

Important in the light of my analysis above, they also conclude:

> Casual empirical evidence suggests to us that only small businesses tend to make efforts to avoid taxes by increasing capital gains through excessive reinvestment of profits and low personal compensation of owners. The economic importance of such small businesses is relatively minor in Hong Kong.

While the conclusions of Hsu and Yuen support the arguments of those in favour of eliminating the capital gains tax in Canada, there are questions about the relevance of evidence drawn from the Hong Kong experience. Hong Kong is unique in many ways. Most important for the present analysis is the fact that the zone's personal income tax rates are about 15% and, therefore, are very low relative to those of most other industrial countries of the world, including Canada. Because of these low personal income tax rates in Hong Kong, the incentives to shift ordinary income into capital gains certainly is less than it would be in countries with higher rates.

On the other hand, this condition raises a point discussed widely among economists. To maximize the incentives for savings and capital formation, which increase economic growth, more of a given amount of revenue should be raised through the increased use of indirect taxes, like value-added taxes and a decreased use of direct taxes, like those on personal and business income. If Canada would adopt such a mix of taxes, its personal income tax rate could be much lower than it is and the incentives to income shifting would be reduced correspondingly.

Switzerland

In *Capital Gains Taxation: Evidence from Switzerland* (p. 55), Peter Kugler and Carlos Lenz note that the federal government of Switzerland does not have a capital gains tax but that such a tax is imposed by some of the cantonal governments. What makes this paper most interesting is that some of these cantonal governments in recent years have abandoned the tax while others have retained it. This virtually controlled experiment has provided important empirical information about the effects of the tax on economic growth. As noted above, the evidence suggests that the cantons without the tax experienced an increase in cantonal income not matched by those cantons that retained the tax.

The authors did not discuss the problems faced by the Swiss government due to the incentives to shift ordinary taxable income into non-taxed capital gains at the federal level. They report that the Swiss federal government has for some time faced political pressures to impose a capital gains tax. However, these pressures have not come from the revenue department or others concerned about the problems created by these incentives. Instead, they have come from the political Left concerned over the large inequalities in wealth and income created by the stock-market boom of the 1990s.

In this sense, Switzerland is like Canada and most of the other industrial countries. Its government faces pressures from citizens with a very static view of the world. These citizens are inclined to focus on income distribution and the living standards of the poor in the short run. They neglect or minimize the negative effect capital gains taxes have on economic growth. Switzerland's per-capita income is one of the highest in the world. According to my analysis presented above, at least some of this higher living standard should be attributed to the historic absence of a capital gains tax at the federal level.

New Zealand

Robin Oliver brings to the writing of his chapter extensive experience as a tax consultant and as an adviser to the revenue department of the government of New Zealand. His chapter, **Capital Gains Tax: The New Zealand Case**, reflects this background. He reports at length on the nature of tax planning and legal maneuvers employed by New Zealanders trying to reduce their tax burden through the shifting of income.

His analysis reflects the conditions that existed in Canada before the introduction of the capital gains tax. As noted in the quotation from Department of Finance 1980 (above, p. 15), these conditions were one of the main justifications for the introduction of the tax in Canada.

Oliver concluded that the zero capital gains tax regime in New Zealand is very costly. There are many lawyers and tax consultants paid to find ways for their clients to avoid taxes through the conversion of other income into capital gains. The government's efforts to prevent these practices in turn results in additional costs. In spite of these government efforts, it is impossible to prevent some tax avoidance, which reduces the efficiency and equity of the entire tax system. It seems that the private sector's ingenuity always finds legal and institutional ways to create new loopholes after old ones have been closed by appropriate changes in government regulations. For these reasons, Oliver recommends the introduction of a capital gains tax in New Zealand:

> I would assert, after my long experience with the New Zealand tax regime as a private consultant and government

adviser, that the best possible system is not one, which simply excludes capital gains from taxable income.

However, he tempers this recommendation by pointing to the particular bias he brings to the issue through his professional background and current position:

> This paper has canvassed the problems posed for New Zealand's tax system by the absence of a general capital gains tax. Undoubtedly, if we had a capital gains tax, the paper would have canvassed the problems posed by having such a tax.

In my view, Oliver's analysis is an important reminder about a fact well known to economists: there is no free lunch. In this sense, his analysis is consistent with the general arguments made above. It reminds us that the merit of moving to a zero capital gains tax rate depends on the outcome of a set of complex calculations. These calculations involve the benefits in terms of greater economic growth against the costs of dealing with attempts to avoid taxes and the effects of incomplete success on the horizontal equity of the system. The weights that analysts put on the costs and benefits are determined to a large extent by their personal and professional backgrounds, which is quite benevolent as long as readers are aware of the analysts' background.

Mexico

Francisco Gil Diaz, the author of *Capital Gains Taxation in Mexico and the Integration of Corporation and Personal Taxes* (p. 89), brings to his analysis a background entirely different from that of Robin Oliver. He holds a PhD in economics from the distinguished University of Chicago. Under President Roberto Salinas, he served as his country's Minister of Revenue, in which capacity he has been credited with increasing the integrity of the system, lowering taxes, broadening the tax base, and increasing enforcement of tax laws and regulations. When he wrote and presented his paper, he was the chief executive officer of a large telecom company in Mexico. After the election of President Vincente Fox, he was appointed Minister of Finance.

On the issue of capital gains taxation, Diaz takes a different approach, as is evident from the following, selective quotations.

If distributed profits and capital gains are taxed differently, people will tend to engage in tax arbitrage and to choose the lower taxed vehicle. Therefore, the correct, neutral and equitable goal is not a favored treatment for capital gains, but rather to strive for a symmetrical treatment of distributed profits and of capital gains. If the first are taxed twice so should the other and, if the first are not adjusted for inflation, it is not clear why the other should.

On the other hand there are no efficiency or equity grounds to double tax corporate profits, if dividend and corporate profit taxation were integrated, that is, if only the individual shareholder were considered the unit of taxation, capital gains taxation would virtually disappear.

Under such a scheme a corporate income tax is solely an individual income tax withheld at the source, just as it is frequently done with wage or interest income. In this vein, individuals add-up their various sources of income, including dividends, albeit grossed-up to determine the before corporate income tax profit, but then the corporate income tax would be creditable as a withheld tax in order to arrive at the individual income tax.

The end result of this procedure is that corporate profits would be taxed only once at the individual's level. Such a design requires parallel corrections in the way capital gains are taxed. The seller of a share would be allowed to modify its purchase price when calculating the difference between the sale and purchase prices to arrive at the taxable capital gain. The required adjustment would be to allow for taxed reinvested profits to be added to the purchase price of the share and to deduct corporate losses.

However transparent and non-distorting, the integration solution has serious drawbacks. The accounting requirements are complex and many years of information and documentation are needed.

Diaz expands on these problems of information and documentation and refers to several issues arising from the policy of taxing personal and business incomes at different rates, which was introduced recently under President Zedillo's regime. However, it appears that Diaz strongly supports eliminating double taxation of business income and, implicitly, the elimination of capital gains taxation.

New Zealand, like Mexico, has a fully integrated system of taxation for personal and business income. It also does not have a capital gains tax. The reasoning of Mexico's Minister of Finance and the experience of New Zealand should be studied carefully. In my view, such a study will increase the support in Canada for the elimination of the capital gains tax and the double taxation of business income.

Inflation indexing

The preceding analysis implies that Canadians would gain large benefits from the elimination of the capital gains tax. However, if such a policy is not adopted, the following analysis suggests ways in which the present system can be made more efficient, transparent, and equitable.

Logical consistency is not the hallmark of the Canadian or any other country's system of taxation. Thus, the argument that a buck is a buck implies that capital gains should fully enter taxable income. There is no reason why capital gains should be treated the way they are in 2001—taxable at only one half of their value. After all, there is no analogous adjustment to wage income or dividends and interest and they give rise to a buck just as capital gains do.

So why are 50% of all capital gains in Canada excluded from taxable income? The official reason is that this practice eliminates the unfairness and inefficiencies resulting from inflation. To see the importance of these considerations consider someone who owns stocks bought at 100. Assume that the general inflation over the following 10 years has doubled the price level and wages so that the real income of the investor and of every other worker remained constant in inflation-adjusted real terms. Now assume that the value of the stocks also doubled to 200 and that they are sold for a realized and taxable gain of 100.

The taxation of these purely nominal gains in that year results in a decrease in the investor's real income. This outcome is not the intention of the capital gains tax legislation but is due to the taxation of phantom capital gains caused by general inflation. In the context of the analogy used above, the holding of the stocks has not produced a taxable fruit and the tax on the nominal gains falls entirely on the tree. In terms of the populist slogan, a buck really is not a buck unless the capital gains are adjusted for inflation.

The logical method for handling problems of inflation is to adjust nominal values correspondingly. However, for reasons that are not clear to me, to adjust for inflation the government of Canada has decided instead to use a blanket approach. All capital gains presently are subject to a 50% inclusion rate. The remaining capital gains then become part of total taxable income and are subject to the investor's personal marginal income tax rate.

It is easy to see that, by the standards of the buck-is-a-buck principle, the 50% inclusion rate results in a fair and efficient adjustment only when over the investors' holding periods the cumulative inflation is exactly 50%. For any given level of inflation, this rule clearly favours capital gains made in the short run. Consider an annual, average inflation rate of 3%. An asset sold after one year is over-compensated for the inflation. On the other hand, at that inflation rate, nominal asset values increasing at the same rate double in 24 years. Assets held over 24 years bring nominal capital gains greater than is compensated for by the 50% inclusion rate.

It is interesting to note that the Canadian system of adjusting for inflation encourages the realization of capital gains in the short run. The United States and many other countries have systems designed to tax short-term more heavily than long-term gains. This approach is used to reduce the magnitude of short-term speculative bubbles in stock and real estate markets.

The injustice created by the broad approach to inflation adjustment for capital gains may be illustrated by an example from recent Canadian history. Between 1972 and 1991, consumer prices in Canada rose 3.8 times while the Toronto Stock Exchange Index of 300 Companies rose 2.9 times. As a result, consider what happened to the financial conditions of a person who bought a representative sample of stocks in the TSI worth $100,000 in 1972. This investment in 1991 was worth $290,000. Its sale that year brought a capital gain of $190,000 and, at the 50% inclusion rate, resulted in taxable income of $95,000. Assume that the gain was taxable at the investor's 50% marginal tax rate on personal income and resulted in a tax payment of $47,500. The investor was left with $242,500 from the sale of the stocks. However, because of the inflation, the real goods and services worth $100,000 in 1972 cost $380,000 in 1991. Our investor suffered a loss of 36.2% of the initial wealth in 1972.

This loss in real wealth has two components. First, there is a decline of 24% due to the excess of the rate of inflation over the growth in the asset value experienced during the years from 1971 to 1992. The second component of 12.2% was due to the tax paid on the fictitious capital gains during the period. Whereas the government cannot control the real decline in asset values directly, it could eliminate the unfair taxation of phantom gains.

To achieve this objective, the Government of Canada needs to index all gains to the actual rate of inflation. This can be done very simply by sending to all taxpayers a table that allows them to read off the cumulative inflation in the consumer price index experienced during the time they bought and sold their assets. Taxpayers can easily adjust their capital losses correspondingly. Under such a system of indexation, the present 50% inclusion rate should rationally be raised to 100%. The outcome of these policy changes would be a fair, efficient, and transparent system of capital gains taxation fully consistent with the principle underlying the slogan that a buck is a buck.

It is possible that such a policy would raise effective rates of capital gains taxation in the future and that it might have meant higher rates in the past compared with what they were under existing 50% inclusion rates and actual inflation. Unfortunately, the estimation of such revenue effects is complicated by the need to make assumptions about the length of holding periods as well as by the assumed rates of future inflation. I have not seen any estimates of this sort made by private scholars though the task should not be beyond the capability of the Canadian government.

The indexing and the full inclusion of capital gains may result in politically undesirable changes in revenues and tax burdens. Under these conditions, revenues can be kept unchanged through the adoption of the American system, which has a special rate for capital gains completely separate from the personal income tax and has generally lower rates for long-term than it has for short-term capital gains. Under this approach, the progressivity of the present Canadian capital gains tax would be eliminated. However, because of the close integration of the two countries' financial markets, the adoption of the same rate in the two countries would provide desirable incentives for the efficient allocation of capital.

Capital gains taxes in the United States are not adjusted for inflation. This has led Alan Greenspan, the Chairman of Board of Governors of the Federal Reserve in Washington to make the following statement:

> Actually I'd go to indexing. And the reason I would is that it's really wrong to tax a part of a gain in assets which are attributable to a decline in the purchasing power of the currency, which is attributable to poor governmental economic policy. So, for the government to tax peoples' assets which rise as a consequence of inferior actions on the part of government strikes me as most inappropriate. (quoted in Joint Economic Committee 1999: 35)

If Canada taxed capital gains tax at the same rate as the United States and if they were indexed, investors would be induced to place more of their capital in Canada. From a narrow Canadian point of view, this would be a desirable development because it would raise the country's capital stock and productivity of labour. The Canadian policy might also give more urgency and weight to Greenspan's recommendation and cause the United States to adopt inflation indexing.

What is the evidence from abroad? Countries with inflation indexing

The indexing of capital gains to inflation is seen by many to cause costly administrative complexities. Three chapters in this volume consider indexing in Britain, Ireland, and Australia.

All three authors conclude that, at the level of individual tax payers, the indexing of capital gains is not a very complex process. As already noted, taxpayers face the simple task of using a table, which the government provides, together with general tax forms and instructions. The table allows taxpayers to read off the amount of inflation in the country in the years elapsed between the initial purchase of the asset and the realization of the gains. The actual calculation of the real taxable gain is very simple and involves the multiplication of two numbers.

However, as in most seemingly simple forms of taxation, there are many devils in the details. These devils often stem from the need to translate a principle into operational instructions for taxpayers. More often they originate with revenue authorities and politicians. Some of the details are introduced in response to the need to counter avoidance techniques used by taxpayers. Some are due to changes in the environment like high levels of inflation, which led to indexation in Britain in the early 1980s. Others are introduced by politicians dissatisfied with the economic and social effects of existing legislation.

United Kingdom

In *Capital Gains Taxation in Britain: The Merit of Indexing and Tapering* (p. 107), Barry Bracewell-Milnes notes that the indexation of capital gains was introduced in 1982 largely in reponse to the economic distortions and inequities caused by the inflation of the late 1970s, which peaked at over 25%. The system of indexation was gradually made more comprehensive. In 1985, it was extended to cover losses. One important operational problem involved the calculation of gains on assets in a portfolio, which were acquired at different prices and times. Until 1982 investors could use the FIFO (first in, first out) principle. Thereafter, they were required to use LIFO (last in, first out) accounting. There was also a rule for averaging prices, which lasted until 1998.

In 1998, indexation was replaced by a system of tapering under which the taxable percentage of a nominal capital gain was made a decreasing function of the time over which the asset was held. Under this rule, only 25% of any gain was taxable if a business asset was held for 10 or more years. This means that a person with a high marginal tax rate effectively pays only a 10% capital gains tax rate. For non-business assets, the maximum effect of tapering is much less generous and makes taxable 60% of gains after 10 years. The 10-year period was reduced to 4 years for business assets in 2000.

The author's view on indexation in his own words is:

> Income and capital gains are as distinct as day and night, even though there are short periods of ambiguity at dawn and dusk. If it were right to tax capital gains as income, indexation would merely remove the additional burden imposed by price

rises. But I believe that it is not right to tax capital gains as income. In my view, therefore, indexation is a means of lightening the burden of an excessive and damaging tax. As such, it reduces public demands for the elimination of the unjust tax and it prevents the adoption of superior alternative methods like tapering for reducing the burden.

The following is the author's final, summary conclusion:

The main thesis of the present paper is that capital gains taxation is an economically damaging tax. Short of the ideal of its abolition, the damage done by the tax can be mitigated by measures to reduce its burden and inefficiencies, like indexation or tapering.

However, these two measures do not have equal merit. Those who view capital gains tax as necessary for reasons of equity and efficiency consider indexation desirable. Indexation makes the tax fairer and less distorting. Tapering generally appeals to those who believe it desirable to have low rates of taxation to minimize the efficiency cost, especially the lock-in effect. Tapering, which ultimately lowers the tax to zero appeals most to those who oppose the Simons definition of income. These analysts, including myself, believe that capital gains are distinctly different from other sources of income and in particular that all certain gains should be taxed and uncertain gains should not.

Australia (Freebairn)

John Freebairn is an economist at the University of Melbourne, specializing in public finance and taxation. In his chapter, **Indexation and Australian Capital Gains Taxation** (p. 123), he notes that Australia adopted a capital gains tax in 1985 mostly to broaden the tax base and eliminate the tax avoidance maneuvers used to avoid paying income and profits taxes. The 1985 law allowed realized capital gains to be adjusted for inflation during the holding period of the asset. Real gains were taxable fully at the payer's personal income-tax rate.

In 1999, indexation was abandoned and Australia adopted a system equivalent to that used in Canada—only one-half of realized gains was taxed at the personal income-tax rate of the owner. Why was indexing abandoned? According to Freebairn, it was not because of any problems inherent in the system:

> The indexing of capital gains for inflation to determine real capital gains is a trivial and low cost exercise once the data on acquisition costs and sales values are known. The Australian Taxation Office provides taxpayers with a table of the general consumer price index along with instructions on how it has to be used. For this reason, high compliance costs associated with the measurement of real capital gains, as opposed to nominal capital gains, has not been a part of any discussions about changes to the Australian system of capital gains taxation.

The reason for the change from indexation to the lower inclusion rate is found in *The Review of Business Taxation*, quoted by Freebairn:

> Though indexation provides a significant reduction in effective rate for many taxpayers, this is probably not well recognized, especially among foreign investors. Indeed the perception has been that the Australian tax system imposes tax at full income tax rates. Such perceptions are not easily corrected and a change in the form of concession or something more akin to the types of concessions available abroad would, in the Review's judgement, be more effective in attracting investors to Australian assets.

The concluding section of Freebairn's paper provides the following assessment of the effects of the 1999 tax reforms:

> The stated objectives of these reforms of the capital gains tax were to encourage innovation, promote domestic and overseas investment in Australian business and achieve greater equity. It is not clear that these objectives of the reform will be achieved. Their attainment depends on questionable assumptions about the rationality of investors, especially that they do not understand the benefits of indexing and put great weight on the fact that only one half of their nominal capital gains are taxable.

The shift from indexing to the halving of the inclusion rate affects the effective tax burden and government revenues in ways discussed above and elaborated on by Freebairn. If, over any given holding period, cumulative inflation exceeds 50% of the nominal capital gain, effective tax rates and revenues are increased. If inflation is below 50%, they are reduced. Since future inflation is not known, it is impossible to know whether the 1999 capital gains tax reforms have increased or lowered effective rates.

Ireland

Capital Gains Taxation in Ireland (p. 141) by Moore McDowell contains a long and detailed history of capital gains taxation in Ireland. Readers will find it interesting how the details of the tax code changed frequently in response to external developments, changes in economic theory, and new political trends. Of greatest interest to the present analysis is the country's experience with inflation indexing:

> The high inflation rates of the 1970s resulted in high capital gains taxes on assets held for long periods. In response to protest over this unfair tax, some major changes in the original capital gains tax regime were introduced. The first of these was in 1978 an inflation adjustment mechanism designed to limit the tax liability to changes in the real rather than the monetary value of assets. This adjustment took the form of what was termed an "inflation multiplier," which was simply the percentage change in the Consumer Price Index in the year up to the beginning of the current financial year beginning on April 6. In practice, the procedure requires an increase in the purchase value of assets by the rate of inflation. The resultant adjusted purchase value is subtracted from the disposal value to arrive at the taxable capital gain.
>
> The 1978 Finance Act also introduced differential tax treatments depending on the length of time an asset had been held. This arrangement can be seen as a form of inflation relief, which already had been granted through the inflation multiplier provision just discussed. So, why was it considered necessary to add this new provision? The authorities offered the argument that the capital gains tax was a disincentive to long term "genuine" investment. Such investment was needed

to encourage capital formation, which would relieve Ireland's chronic problem of underemployment and foster structural change needed in the wake of accession to membership in the European Economic Community. On the other hand, accruals of wealth based on mere "speculation" were considered to be a legitimate target of taxation on the grounds of equity. Since assets held for longer time periods were already subject to inflation indexing, the lower rate of taxation for them means that were over-compensated for inflation.

McDowell explains some fundamental and sophisticated theoretical issues raised by the practice of indexation. Readers must judge for themselves the extent to which these criticisms imply that inflation indexing is economically undesirable.

References

Department of Finance (1980). A Review of the Taxation of Capital Gains in Canada–An Examination of the Canadian Experience and of Issues Involved in Proposals for Change (November).

Grubel, Herbert (2000). *Unlocking Canadian Capital: The Case for Capital Gains Tax Reform*. Vancouver, BC: The Fraser Institute.

Haig, R.M. (1921). *The Federal Income Tax*. New York: Columbia University Press.

Joint Economic Committee (1999). The Budget, Taxation, and Economic Growth. Staff Report, Growth and Prosperity Series (October). Washington, DC: Joint Economic Committee.

Organisation for Economic Cooperation and Development (1997). *Economic Surveys, Canada*. Paris: OECD.

Porter, Michael (1980). *Competitive Strategy: Techniques for analysing industries and competitors*. New York: Free

———, Richard Caves, Michael Spence, with John Scott (1988). *Competition in the Open Economy: A Model Applied to Canada*, Cambridge, MA: Harvard University Press.

Romer, Paul (1986). Increasing Returns and Long-Run Growth. *Journal of Political Economy* 94 (October): 1002–37.

Simons, H.C. (1938). *Personal Income Taxation*. Chicago: University of Chicago Press.

Spindler, Zane (2001). Public Choice versus Public Finance on the Social Costs of Capital Gains Tax: An Expository Note. Unpublished manuscript obtainable from the author at Simon Fraser University or the University of Cape Town.

Tullock, Gordon (1967). The Welfare Costs of Tariffs, Monopolies, and Theft. *Western Eonomic Journal* 5: 224–32.

Wanniski, Jude (1999). *Lesson 17: Taxing Capital Gains*. Supply-Side University Spring Semester Lesson #17. Digital document: www.polyconomics.com/showarticle.asp?articleid=295 (as of September 18, 2001).

2 Capital gains tax regimes abroad—countries without capital gains taxes

Tax avoidance due to the zero capital gains tax

Some indirect evidence from Hong Kong

BERRY F. C. HSU AND CHI-WA YUEN

Consistent with its image as a free-market economy with minimal government intervention, Hong Kong is a city with low and simple taxation. Unlike most industrial and developed economies with full-fledged tax structures, Hong Kong has a relatively narrow tax base. It has direct taxes, which account for about 60% of the total tax revenue. These direct levies fall on earnings and profits and include an estate duty. Hong Kong also has indirect taxes, which account for the remaining 40%. These consist of rates, duties, and taxes on motor vehicles and so on.[1] Nonetheless, Hong Kong has neither a sales or value-added tax nor a capital gains tax. In this paper, we explain the absence of the capital gains tax and provide some indirect evidence on the tax-avoidance effects induced by this fact.

Notes will be found on pages 51–53.

Why is there no capital gains tax in Hong Kong?

Under the British colonial rule, no tax was levied on capital gains in Hong Kong.[2] This continues to be the case since the Chinese government took over in 1997.

During the pre-1997 (colonial) period, the tax structure in Hong Kong was based on the British tax system, which uses the *source* concept of income for the taxation of different kinds of income. This concept originated in Great Britain in the late eighteenth century. It argues that only incomes derived from identifiable sources—rather than the sources themselves—are subject to tax. In this sense, income generated by a capital asset is taxable while the capital asset itself is not.

Historically, countries with common-law regimes have adhered to the source concept and have not had capital gains taxation. However, there are a few exceptions to this rule. Capital gains are taxed in Australia, Canada, and Great Britain, all of which are common-law jurisdictions. The capital gains taxes in these countries are justified on the highly debatable ground that capital gains are a part of capital income, do not represent the source, and therefore are taxable even if the source principle is followed. This is one of the few areas where the Hong Kong tax system diverges from its British counterpart. In this sense, history and convention alone cannot explain the absence of the capital gains tax in Hong Kong.

After the 1997 hand-over, the *Basic Law* provided for the retention by the Hong Kong Special Administrative Region (HKSAR) of the tax structure already existing.[3] Until recently, the fiscal budgets in Hong Kong have been surplus prone.[4] Thus, there has been little need for the government to introduce new taxes—including a capital gains tax—to finance its expenditures. The taxing authority has not given any official explanation for the absence of that tax and no tax reform or review committees have been created to look into the issue.[5, 6] Circumstantial evidence suggests that the main reason for not introducing the capital gains tax stems from the HKSAR government's obsession with the simplicity and efficiency of the existing low tax policy—even at the expense of the no less important principles of vertical and horizontal equity. However, the reluctance to introduce a capital gains tax may also be due to the well-known problems of valuing capital assets, avoiding the lock-in effects, and eliminating inflation-induced distortions, which accompany the administration of the tax.

Although there is no capital gains tax in the HKSAR, there are two distinct types of taxes on capital. They fall on property rather than on gains from property, and they are levied under different conditions. First, stamp duties are charged on documents relating to the transfer of certain types of property (e.g., leases, shares, and immovable properties). Second, estate duties are a form of inheritance tax imposed on the value of property located in the HKSAR and passed on to heirs at the death of a person. Stamp duties bring in more than 10% of the total operating revenue for the government whereas estate duties account for only 1%.

Trading profits versus capital gains

The absence of the capital gains tax does not mean that all incomes generated in the process of asset transactions are tax-free. Under section 14 of the Inland Revenue Ordinance, the profits tax expressly excludes "profits arising from the sale of capital assets" (i.e., profits from *capital* sources). More precisely, such a sale must involve "assets." But, profits arising otherwise than from "the sale of capital assets" are not excluded from profits tax liability.

There is, however, no legal authority to impose tax on these profits either, unless they arise in the ordinary course of a "trade, profession, or business." The exclusion provided by this provision is to avoid doubt more than anything else. What constitutes a "sale" and what is an "asset" are nonetheless not always clear. On the other hand, profits arising from a trade or the practice of professions (i.e., profits from *non-capital* sources, or profits of a revenue nature) are taxed. In addition, a tax may be charged on the profits of speculative transactions if they can be shown to constitute an adventure in the nature of trade.[7]

Problems arise when assets are traded as a matter of routine business, as in the case of a real estate firm specializing in the purchase and resale of buildings and land. Profits from such trade in assets are taxable. In principle, profits from the increase in the value of such property held as trading inventory are not taxable. In practical law, however, the concept of "trade" has not been precisely defined in the Inland Revenue Ordinance. As a result, courts are often asked to adjudicate disputes between citizens who claim that income is from capital gains rather than from trade and the tax authorities who argue that the income is due to trading.

Hong Kong courts have often been asked to rule on such ambiguities. These rulings constitute the common-law base for deciding whether a particular transaction is a trade or involves a capital gain. Six basic factors called "the badges of trade" have emerged from these rulings and have been summarized in the *Final Report* published in 1955 by the British Royal Commission on the Taxation of Profits and Income. The "badges of trade" considered by courts are:

(1) the subject matter of realization,

(2) the length of the period of ownership,

(3) the frequency or number of similar transactions by the same person,

(4) supplementary work on, or in connection with, the property realized,

(5) the circumstances that were responsible for the realization,

(6) the motive for the realization.

It is beyond the scope of this paper to discuss trade in greater detail. For our purpose, it is sufficient to note that many appeals concerning profits tax assessment by the Inland Revenue Department are related to disputes over the issue whether profits earned are trading profits (which are taxable) or capital gains (which are tax-exempt). Almost always, the verdict whether a transaction is deemed to have given rise to a taxable profit is based on the "badges of trade" test.

Tax avoidance and the Hong Kong Inland Revenue board of review

Although there is no capital gains tax in the HKSAR, in the 1998/1999 fiscal year, tax on gains from the property sector accounted for 32% of the total profits tax collected (equivalent to 14% of total government tax revenue). Together with revenues from stamp duty and estate duty, tax on capital-related income accounted for some 25.5% of the total tax revenue. Accordingly, there is a very strong incentive for taxpayers to shift their income into capital gains while adhering to anti-avoidance provisions in the code.

Believing in the basic principle of simplicity, the Inland Revenue Ordinance from the outset has been designed to contain very little strict anti-avoidance legislation. However, over time, the growth of sophisticated tax planning arrangements has led to the introduction of many sub-sections in the Inland Revenue Ordinance aimed at closing loopholes. Now the Inland Revenue Ordinance contains two general anti-avoidance provisions. The first sets out to disregard any "artificial or fictitious" transactions that do not, in fact, take place and any that reduce or would reduce the amount of tax payable. The second applies the test of "sole or dominant purpose" to determine whether a transaction is conducted mainly for the purpose of obtaining tax benefits through the avoidance or postponement of the liability to pay tax or the reduction in the amount thereof.

Among the specific anti-avoidance provisions of the Inland Revenue Ordinance, the most relevant to our analysis is section 15A. It is intended to counteract the following type of transaction. A person sells the right to a stream of taxable income to another person for a lump sum. This lump sum is claimed to be a tax-free capital gain. However, as long as the seller retains the ownership of the underlying asset, such a lump-sum sale of a stream of income is deemed to have been undertaken to avoid the payment of income taxes on the income and the alleged capital gain is taxed as income. Such an arrangement was the subject of a legal procedure in Australia (*FC of T v. Myer Emporium Ltd.* (85 ATC 411)). Initially a court held that the receipt was indeed of the nature of a capital gain and thus not taxable. However, a higher court in Australia later reversed that decision on appeal.[8] The money received through the transaction was considered to be trading profit and hence taxable. Although the court decision has become a common-law precedent, section 15A of the Inland Revenue Ordinance code has been retained to avoid any ambiguities.

In fact, the court decision and section 15A have not prevented attempts to avoid taxes through transactions that turn income into non-taxable capital gains. This is, at least in part, due to the fact that it is not always clear whether a given transaction is designed to avoid taxes or whether it is a genuine commercial activity that only appeared to involve tax evasion. As a result, a number of rulings by the Commissioner of Inland Revenue that specific transactions are for tax avoidance have been appealed to the Board of Review of the Hong Kong Inland Revenue. These appeals may be considered to reflect the extent to which the absence of a capital-gains tax has induced shifting of ordinary income into capital gains.

Table 1 contains some statistics about appeals to the Board of Review against the decisions made by the Commissioner of Inland Revenue that the transactions involved were revenue in nature (hence, taxable) rather than capital in nature (hence, not taxable). The table also distinguishes whether these appeals involved transactions in land or other assets. Note that under the statutes of the Board of Review, the onus of proving that the receipts are capital in nature rests with the appellant taxpayers.

The second column in the table shows in parenthesis the total number of appeals filed in the years concerned. The numbers reveal that about 40% of the appeals are related specifically to the dispute about "revenue versus capital" or "profits versus capital gains." Table 1 also shows that during the three years under consideration, in cases involving land, more than 3 times as many appeals (49) were dismissed than were allowed (15). In the case of non-land the ratio was 2.1, with 85 appeals dismissed and 40 allowed. Although we have not reported data on the values of the transactions involved in these appeals, the high rates of unsuccessful appeals suggest that many taxpayers would have devised schemes to avoid tax liabilities by shifting their assets from trading stock to capital. Had they been successful, there would be substantial tax savings.[9]

In this context, it is worth noting that taxpayers filing appeals face fees charged by lawyers and accountants, which tend to be small relative to the gains expected from a favourable ruling. At the same

Table 1: Appeals to the Board of Review

	Total number of cases	Appeal dismissed Land	Appeal dismissed Non-land	Appeal allowed Land	Appeal allowed Non-land
1997	54 (out of 126)	12	23	8	11
1998	77 (out of 179)	25	29	7	16
1999	58 (out of 152)	12	33	0	13

Source: Board of Review Decisions 1997–99.

time, the downside risk of an unfavourable ruling is also relatively small. The assessed tax has to be paid and the amount is the same as it would have been without the appeal. Furthermore, the Board imposes only rarely a deterrent penalty of US$640, which in principle is payable upon unfavourable Board rulings. For these reasons, we believe that taxpayers have strong incentives to appeal. Therefore, the numbers in the table represent a reasonable estimate of the number of times Inland Revenue agents decide to rule against taxpayers and force them to treat claimed capital gains as taxable other income.

However, this conclusion is mitigated to some degree by the fact that some taxpayers do not go to the appeal board and instead settle their perceived grievances through direct deals with the Inland Revenue Department. They have strong incentives to do so since the Department has the authority to impose a penalty on incorrect returns of up to three times the tax owed. Unfortunately, there are no estimates of the number and value of appealed rulings settled through direct dealings with the Inland Revenue Department.

Techniques for converting income into capital gains

The most popular technique used in converting ordinary income into non-taxable capital gains involves the use of "creative" accounting. This practice is limited by the fact that under the Companies Ordinance auditors must certify accounting documents to show a "true and fair view" of the company's affairs. Auditors have some room for subjective view of such conditions to suit a client's interest but the actions based on such views must comply with accepted accounting standards.

Of course, such compliance can be ambiguous and can lead to legal challenges. For example, in Case No. D180/98 it was alleged that with the approval of an auditor, a taxpayer shifted property from trading to capital in the "current assets" account in 1991, 8 years after its acquisition. The taxpayer argued that this accounting measure was proper since the original acquisition of the asset as a trading property had been a mistake from the very beginning and, since it was not sold after 8 years, it had become a balance-sheet asset. The Inland Revenue Department argued that there was a change of intention only after the taxpayer failed to find a purchaser.

The Board of Review held that there must be strong evidence to substantiate a mistake. After considering all the surrounding circumstances, it concluded that the taxpayer's transfer of the property from trading stock to capital took effect on the date upon which the revaluation of the property was based, i.e., 1991 instead of 1983 (the acquisition date). This revaluation, which was done in 1991 rather than 1983, would be unnecessary had there not been a change of intention. In other words, while the conversion was granted, the taxpayer would still have to pay taxes due to the change in the property's value between 1983 (when it was treated as a trading asset) and 1991 (when it was reclassified as a long-term fixed asset). In relation to this revaluation issue, see also the discussion about *Sharkey v. Wernher* below.

As another example of a strategy used to convert income into capital gains that led to a legal challenge, consider case No. D108/97. In this case a taxpayer claimed to have acquired a property for building for use as storage facility (which made it an investment for general business purposes) because of the serious traffic problems he was facing in existing storage spaces. However, the taxpayer encountered a change of cost conditions that made it infeasible to use the property for storage. The property was sold and claimed to have resulted in a capital gain. The taxpayer submitted evidence in the form of reports from chartered surveyors used to plan the construction of the storage and also submitted detailed statistical evidence on planned sales and logistics.

The cost of preparing this evidence was insignificant in relation to the tax savings realized if the sale was considered to have resulted in a capital gain rather than taxable income from ordinary business investment. The Board of Review argued that the taxpayer had to prove that his intention was genuine, realistic, and realizable. It dismissed the appeal on the grounds that the estimated traffic congestion was unrealistic and the change in business environment not valid as a reason for changing the intended use of the property.

Another example of the importance of accounting records in determining whether income constitutes a capital gain is found in Case No. D64/98. In this case, one firm compensated another for the early termination of an agreement to distribute capital goods. The recipient of the funds claimed that this payment was a non-taxable capital gain. The payer of the funds claimed it as a loss, which should reduce its income for tax purposes. The Board of Review agreed with the firm receiving the money because it was mere coincidence that the present value formula used to estimate the compensation (a stock) yielded a level that was roughly equal to one-year's foregone profit of the distributor (a flow). It went on to argue that the early termination of the distribution contract was a loss or sterilization of the taxpayer's capital asset. It amounted to an enduring destruction of its profit-making potential. The compensation payment was therefore a once-only capital gain, which compensated for this loss. By the same token, the Board decided that the payer of the compensation could not claim the payment as business losses for tax purposes.

Difficulties in deciding whether a transaction gives rise to capital gains or ordinary income can arise when the shift of assets from trading to capital uses takes place while the ownership of the property has not changed. According to a legal precedent (*Sharkey v. Wernher*), the property should be revalued at the time it is shifted. The value is to be determined by applying the doctrine of imputed income from trading use and compared its value as a capital asset to determine whether there is taxable profit involved. But arguably this doctrine is not applicable when the taxpayer is in only one type of business and there is no real change in the services derived from the asset by redefining it as capital.

In *Commissioner of Inland Revenue v. Quitsubdue*, the Board of Review held that there was a change of intention by the taxpayer when trading stock was converted into fixed assets; but that, since the property in question had never been disposed of by the taxpayer, there was no profit. The Court of First Instance said *obiter* that *Sharkey* could not generally apply in the HKSAR because a person cannot trade with himself and earn a profit in the process. In this case, the property had always been in the possession of the same enterprise.

It is interesting to note that in *Sharkey* the taxpayer transferred racehorses from her stud farm to her racing stables, which were separate taxing entities and the exchange did not strictly involve a trade with oneself. It was a misfortune that the Court of First Instance did not address this distinction.

In many appeals, the taxpayer would argue that the sale of an asset is related to a long-term or permanent investment and gives rise to a non-taxable capital gain. In Case No. D28/98, a private limited company claimed that it had initially intended to acquire a property as a long-term investment for use as an office for the company. Profits arising from the subsequent sale of this property should be treated as a capital gain. The Board found the taxpayer's explanations for the sale of the property somewhat contradictory and dismissed the appeal. This was a clear case in which the taxpayer tried to exploit the absence of the capital gains tax to avoid the tax on profits, which had arisen from an ordinary business deal.

In Case No. D117/97, a taxpayer took out a mortgage of HK$4,000,000 to purchase a property worth HK$8,500,000. Within half a year, the property was sold for HK$11,650,000. The Board decided that this transaction involved speculative trading rather than an investment. The profits were subject to income taxation.

All of the preceding cases involved real estate property. But, as table 1 reveals, there were also quite a few non-land cases. In Case No. D113/98, for instance, a private, incorporated company was engaged in retail and wholesale business. It sold shares of two listed companies operating in the property sector and argued that these shares had originally been acquired as long-term investments so that profits from the sale should be treated as non-taxable gains rather than taxable profits. The appeal was dismissed by the Board on the ground that the shares were claims on firms whose business was unrelated to that of the taxpayer. It rejected the taxpayer's claim of being on the constant lookout for good investments in its own areas of business and ordered that the profits from the sale of the shares gave rise to taxable trading income

There are many more cases of similar nature. We believe, though, that these examples are sufficient to illustrate the main methods used by Hong Kong taxpayers to avoid the payment of income taxes by converting income from trading into non-taxable capital gains.

Conclusions

In the absence of capital gains taxes, businesses and private taxpayers have incentives to shift taxable profits or incomes into non-taxable capital gains. These practices reduce economic efficiency and cause inequities in the incidence of taxes. However, direct evidence on the frequency and quantitative importance of such practices is impossible to obtain because by the very nature of the transactions, they are highly confidential and unpublicized.

In this paper, we used some indirect evidence to assess the extent of the shifting of other income into non-taxable capital gains. We considered appeals to the Board of Review of the Hong Kong Inland Revenue about the classification of income on which the tax is levied as revenue or capital.

Based on this indirect evidence and our common sense about the Hong Kong economy we have reached the following conclusions:

- Few businesses "invest" in properties for the long term or for their own business use. Such investment in real estate is speculative and bets on the soaring property values. The investments have often been financed through mortgage loans rather than retained profits. The returns to such speculative investments were properly treated as taxable profits.

- Before the Asian crisis, when the property market was still booming, the absence of the capital gains tax probably stimulated some businesses to buy office or factory buildings rather than rent them.[10] While some of these investments may have been for the medium or long term, it is disputable whether profits made from their sales should then be considered as non-taxable capital gains.

- Tax avoidance through the claim that purchase of property is long-term investment, hence profit so derived is capital gains, imposes relatively low costs on taxpayers. It is, therefore, attempted by some, but the Revenue authorities often disallow these attempts and the Board of Review tends to uphold these rulings.

- Firms have the option to reinvest earnings and take tax-free capital gains rather than pay tax on the earnings. However, such excessive reinvestment of business earnings by definition implies investment in projects or assets with lower risk-adjusted expected rates of return than can be earned by placing the funds in outside investments. It makes sense only if the gains from tax avoidance exceed the losses from the low-return internal investments. Since personal and corporate income taxes in Hong Kong are very low, the incentives to reinvest earnings and take the implicit losses are relatively minor.

- Casual empirical evidence suggests to us that only small businesses tend to make efforts to avoid taxes by increasing capital gains through excessive reinvestment of profits and low personal compensation of owners. The economic importance of such small businesses is relatively minor in Hong Kong.

On the basis of the indirect evidence available to us we conclude that the absence of a capital gains tax in Hong Kong has resulted in little, if any, inefficiencies and inequities.[11]

Notes

1 Rates are levied on landed properties at a fixed percentage of their ratable value in order to finance the various public services provided by the provisional municipal councils. Duties include stamp duty, betting duty, and duties on four types of commodities (i.e., hydrocarbon oil, alcoholic beverages, methyl and ethyl alcohol, and tobacco).

2 As capital gains are not taxable, capital losses are not tax-deductible either.

3 According to Article 108 of the *Basic Law*, "... [t]he HKSAR shall, taking the low tax policy previously pursued in Hong Kong as reference, enact laws on its own concerning types of taxes, tax rates, tax reductions, allowances and exemptions, and other matters of taxation." For a more detailed description of the background on the HKSAR tax system and the source concept of income, see Hsu (1996) and (2000). See also One Country Two Systems Economic Research Institute Ltd. (1992).

4 For the past two decades, deficits have only been recorded in 5 years, and they were covered by the fiscal reserves accumulated from the surplus years. In keeping with the living-within-our-means rule, the following guiding principles of financial management have been used repeatedly by the financial secretaries in Hong Kong in drawing up budgets: (a) *spending constraints:* public spending should be sufficiently covered by revenue and should not grow faster than the economy; and (b) *adequate reserves:* the fiscal reserves should provide a sufficient cushion to meet known commitments and to guard against future uncertainties. This conservative philosophy has been re-emphasized in Article 107 of the *Basic Law*, according to which "*[t]he HKSAR shall follow the principle of keeping expenditure within the limits of revenues in drawing up its budget, and strive to achieve a fiscal balance, avoid deficits and keep the budget commensurate with the growth rate of its gross domestic product.*"

5 A few years ago, there were some discussions about whether the capital gains tax should be introduced as a device to curb speculative activities in the Hong Kong property market. Despite support from some political parties, many people (economists included) were concerned about the potentially harmful effects of introducing a capital gains tax or some kind of anti-speculation tax on property. A capital gains tax may choke off speculative demand for

housing and bring down property prices in the short run. However, if the capital gains tax rate is sufficiently high, it would ultimately discourage developers from increasing the supply of new housing units, reduce the liquidity of the property market, and perhaps slow down the growth of the whole economy through its negative effect on the property and banking sectors. (For example, see Siu 1997.) It was suggested instead that the surging property prices would be contained better through a long-term policy of increasing land supply, which was actually adopted by the HKSAR government at the time. This so-called "85,000" policy was later abandoned due to the collapse of the property market following the onset of the Asian crisis.

6 Owing to the growing problem of fiscal deficits, the HKSAR government has started to consider measures to broaden its tax base. The introduction of a sales tax is currently under serious consideration but that of the capital gains tax is still not in the picture.

7 Section 2(1) of the Inland Revenue Ordinance provides that "trade includes every trade and manufacture, and every adventure and concern in the nature of a trade." This definition is not exhaustive. Basically, the Ordinance looks for whether the taxpayer engages in an "adventure and concern," which is similar to a trade, or has the nature and special characteristics of a trade. The majority of litigation in this regard is related to transactions involving an "adventure and concern in the nature of a trade." This is a grey area of law on the borderline. Whether a particular activity is a "trade" fundamentally is a question of fact. Members of the Board of Review and judges are only human so that idiosyncrasies inevitably filter into their findings of fact. Therefore, it may sometimes be difficult to reconcile reported cases on the definition of "trade." In *Kowloon Stock Exchange Ltd. v. Commissioner of Inland Revenue*, for instance, the Privy Council adopted the principle that trade denoted "operations of a commercial character by which the trader provides to customers for reward some kind of goods or services." An isolated transaction may trigger "an adventure and concern in the nature of a trade." Accordingly, section 14(1) of the Inland Revenue Ordinance may operate to tax a person even though he does not carry on a "trade" or "manufacture." In *Rutledge v. Inland Revenue Commissioners*, it was held that a one-off transaction without a continuous series of trading operations could trigger a trade.

8 One may wonder why an Australian decision should be relevant to Hong Kong. Article 84 of the *Basic Law* provides that the courts of the HKSAR "... *may refer to precedents of other common law jurisdictions* ..." in adjudication cases.
9 For the transaction of a residential flat of 1,000 sq.ft. at average mid-1990s prices and under a profits tax of 15%, say, such tax-avoiding appeal could easily save the owner a tax liability of HK$900,000.
10 Purchases of residential properties might have further been stimulated by tax-deduction benefits for depreciation allowances and for mortgage payments applied to first-time purchases.
11 It does not, therefore, follow that a zero capital gains tax is totally efficient. As is familiar from the theory of optimal taxation, the inability to collect tax revenue from capital gains implies that some other activities have to be taxed more heavily in order to finance fiscal spending, thus resulting in excessive distortions at other margins.

References

Hsu, Berry F.C. (1996). *A Guide to Hong Kong Taxation*. Hong Kong: Open Learning Institute Press and Chinese University Press.

―――― (2000). A Treatise on the HKSAR Tax Law. Unpublished manuscript. Department of Real Estate and Construction, University of Hong Kong.

One Country Two Systems Economic Research Institute Ltd.(1992). *The Basic Law of the Hong Kong Special Administrative Region of the People's Republic of China*. Hong Kong: One Country Two Systems Economic Research Institute.

Siu, Alan K.F (1997). Capital Gains Tax on Property. Unpublished manuscript. School of Economics and Finance, University of Hong Kong

Capital gains taxation

Evidence from Switzerland

Peter Kugler and Carlos Lenz

Capital gains taxes on the sale of company shares and other so-called movable property, which were collected by most cantons in the past at the household level, were completely abolished in Switzerland in recent years. However, the persistent stock market boom of the 1990s generated pressure by trade unions and the social democratic party to reintroduce capital gains taxation at the confederation level. Nevertheless, the federal government did not include a capital gains tax in its 1998 measures to close loopholes in income taxation. The outbreak of the Asian crisis and the resulting stock-market crash in the autumn of 1998 led to a decreasing interest in capital gains taxation but the stock market recovery of the last two years brought this issue again on to Switzerland's political agenda. The trade unions and the social democratic party recently started an initiative referendum to introduce this tax at the confederation level; the initiative referendum, if supported by a sufficient number of citizens, will be the subject of a future referendum.

In this chapter, we describe the experience of Switzerland with capital gains taxation. First, we discuss briefly the very complex

---

Notes will be found on page 70.

Swiss tax system with its taxes at the confederation, cantonal, and community levels and provide some details concerning taxation of capital income that are of interest in the present context. Second, we present the results of a statistical analysis of the effect on real income and tax revenues at the cantonal level of abolishing capital gains tax in eight cantons between 1986 and 1990. Third, we report the results of an empirical analysis of the determinants of capital gains tax revenue in the canton Basel-Stadt, for which separate capital gains tax data are available for the period from 1965 to 1990. The chapter closes with a summary and conclusions.

Capital gains taxes in the Swiss tax jungle

The Swiss tax system is so complex that some authors called it a tax jungle (Duss and Bird 1979). The system reflects the institutional features of this country: namely, a highly decentralised government structure and direct democracy. In particular, direct taxation (of income and wealth) is very heterogeneous as these taxes are collected by the confederation, the cantons, and the communities at the household and business level according to different schemes with different rates and definitions of the tax base. Indirect taxation is much simpler as the federal (confederation) government only collects the value-added tax (VAT) and there is no overlap among the taxes levied by the different levels of government.

Before turning to the details concerning taxation of capital income, some general remarks on the level and the structure of the Swiss tax revenues are warranted. The total tax burden in Switzerland (including social security) is now over 35%. This value is still lower than in all major continental European countries but higher than that of the United Sates. There was a strong increase in the tax burden in the 1990s, which was greater than the growth of tax revenue in major European countries.

Another important special feature of the Swiss tax system is that it mainly relies on direct taxation. The VAT is collected at a standard rate of 7.5%, which is very low compared to the European Union standard rate of nearly 20%. Thus the tax burden on consumption is low (around 8%) and the effective tax burden on labour (including social security contributions) and capital income (including all business and household taxes on capital income and property as well as financial transactions) is relatively high. According to a recent IMF study by Jaeger, Hviding and Purfield (1999), the effective tax burden[1] on labour has increased from slightly above 30% in 1985 to nearly 40% in 1996. However, this trend is shared with all other major European countries and Switzerland is still one of the countries with the lowest tax burden on labour income in Europe.

It is no longer true that Switzerland has the lowest tax rate for capital income for two reasons. First, many European countries have recently lowered the tax burden on capital income through reforms that reduced the dual taxation of business and household incomes. Second, tax burden on capital income has risen from 28% to 33% since 1985. As a result, only one major European Union country, the United Kingdom, has a higher tax burden on capital income than Switzerland.

A closer look at capital income taxation reveals that the confederation, the cantons, and the communities each tax incorporated businesses and households. Each jurisdiction applies its own taxation scheme, which often differs greatly from that of others. A detailed account of the subject would cover the tax codes of the confederation, 26 cantons, and around 3000 communities. Thus, the following discussion can only give a broad overview of capital income taxation in Switzerland and omits details.[2]

It should be noted that the tax burden varies greatly within the country. Data from 1996 show that in the low-tax canton, Zug, the burden is only 44% of that in the high-tax canton, Jura. This condition is accompanied by large differences in real-estate prices and the levels of public goods provided by the cantonal government. There is also only a limited mobility of labour, caused by language differences,[3] among other things.

Since 1997, company profits are taxed by the confederation at a constant rate of 8.5%. In earlier years, the tax rate was progressive, depending on the ratio of profits to equity. In many cantons, profits are still taxed according to rates depending on this ratio. Only eight cantons levy a constant tax rate on profits. The highest average rates of company profits charged by cantons and communities[4] vary from 12% to 35%, with sometimes strange changes in the marginal rate caused by piecewise linear schemes in profit-to-equity ratios. Thus, cantonal taxes result in some obvious non-neutralities of the tax system, which favour financing investment by equity issues and retained earnings. Moreover, there are marked differences in the tax treatment of investment according to its type and financing. Realized capital gains are taxed in this framework as far as they are reflected in profits.

Households see their capital income taxed again at all three levels of government. Interest and dividends are taxed progressively as part of total family income. The confederation levies taxes at a maximum rate of 11.5% with a very strong progression for family incomes between 60,000 and 150,000 Swiss Francs. The highest income-tax rates imposed by cantons and communities vary greatly from more than 10% to slightly above 30%. Allowable deductions also differ greatly among cantons, which further contributes to a varying income-tax burden. Most cantons and communities collect a progressive wealth tax with a maximum rate ranging from 0.2% to 1%. As mentioned in the introduction, there was capital gains taxation on movable property at the cantonal level in the past, which was collected either as a separate tax or by a corresponding increase in taxable income. Today, a capital gains tax is collected only on capital gains realized through the sale of non-movable property like land and buildings.

The initiative for the introduction of a capital gains tax

At the turn of the millennium, Switzerland faces a political initiative designed to introduce a federal tax on realized capital gains on movable property at a constant rate of 20% to 30%. This political initiative should be seen in the light of many general and widely known arguments against taxing realized capital gains. As Stiglitz (1983) and Grubel (2000) note, such taxes affect the financial behaviour of households and companies, mainly through locking in and locking out invested capital subject to capital gains taxation. In addition, there are many well-known arguments against increasing the tax burden on capital. There is already double taxation of savings, interest, and dividends through taxes imposed on both the incomes of business and persons. Capital is highly mobile internationally and readily leaves countries with high capital taxes for countries with low capital taxes. Thus, further increases in the tax burden on capital may well result in reduced capital formation and real income.

With this general background in mind,[5] we can make the following specific points against the introduction of a capital gains tax on movable property in Switzerland.

First, the effective tax burden on capital is relatively high by international standards and in comparison to that on consumption. In particular, the difference between the effective tax burden on labour and capital is relatively low by international standards. This is clearly a strong argument against the introduction of a capital gains tax as an additional burden on the internationally highly mobile factor capital.

Second, both realized and non-realized capital gains on movable property are already implicitly taxed in the framework of the cantonal and community wealth tax. Assuming a pre-tax rate of return of 5%, a wealth tax of 0.5% implies a 10% tax on all capital gains. Taking into account that only a fraction of capital gains are realized, this figure may well imply an implicit taxation of realized capital gains at a rate between 20% and 30%.

Third, the introduction of the proposed capital gains tax would lead to inefficiencies in the financial behaviour of households and companies in order to avoid this tax. Moreover, this tax would increase the already high administrative costs of the very complex Swiss tax system and is likely to provide relatively low revenues, given the incentives and possibilities to avoid this additional tax.

Empirical evidence on the effects of abolishing capital gains tax in eight cantons from 1986 to 1990

As mentioned in the introduction, until 1996 a capital gains tax on realized gains on movable property existed in most Swiss cantons. As a result, data on income, tax revenues for the years 1986 to 1990 offer a unique opportunity to study empirically the effects of abolishing the capital gains tax. The data are available for the eight cantons of Bern (BE), Basel-Land (BL), Basel-Stadt (BS), Jura (JU), St. Gallen (SG), Solothurn (SO), Thurgau (TG), and Valais (VS).[6] We used these data for the following analysis.

Effects on income

First, we checked whether abolishing the capital gains tax led to a break in the deterministic trend in real cantonal national income, which was obtained by deflating nominal income by the consumer price index.[7] We used a log linear trend model with a break in 1990, accounting for the prolonged stagnation of the Swiss economy in the 1990s. The abolishment of the capital gains tax was represented by an additional dummy variable, which takes the value one from the year of abolishment onwards. Lagged adjustment of real income to its trend level is represented by the lagged endogenous variable. The system for all eight cantons was estimated with annual data covering the period from 1978 to 1995 by the Seemingly Unrelated Regression method.

Second, we did the same exercise for the real direct tax revenue of the eight cantons. Nominal tax revenue is deflated by the consumer price index.

The results from our regressions for the canton income data are presented in table 1. As can be seen, all cantons exhibit a strong break in the slope of the trend function at the beginning of the 1990s. In our context, we are mainly interested in the estimates of the coefficient of the capital gains taxation dummy variable. For seven of the cantons,[8] the estimate is positive, statistically significantly different from zero in most cases and is about the same size for all cantons. The same result holds for the coefficient of the lagged dependent variable. Statistical tests of the hypothesis that these coefficients are the same across cantons cannot be rejected since the corresponding chi-squared values reported in table 1 are below the critical value for any reasonable significance level. The estimation results for the accordingly restricted system are reported in table 2. The coefficient of the dummy variable for the abolishment of the capital gains tax is statistically highly significant. The long-run effect calculated with the coefficient estimate of the lagged dependent variable amounts to 3.2%.

The data presented in tables 1 and 2 suggest that abolishing the capital gains tax has had positive and economically significant effects on the *level* of real income in the cantons. According to the New Growth Theory, abolishing the capital gains tax should also raise the growth rate of real income.[9] Our data suggest that if there is such an effect on the growth rate, it is too small to be detected

Table 1: Effect of capital gains tax on real national income, 1978–1995: Unrestricted estimates

$$y_{it} = \beta_{i1}C_{7890} + \beta_{i2}T_{7890} + \beta_{i3}C_{9195} + \beta_{i4}T_{9195} + \beta_{i5}D_{AKGS} + \beta_{i6}y_{i,t-1}$$

i	β_{i1}	β_{i2}	β_{i3}	β_{i4}	β_{i5}	β_{i6}	$\dfrac{\beta_{i5}}{1-\beta_{i6}}$	$\overline{R}^2$	D.W.	SEE
BE	9.15	0.0137	9.43	−0.0089	0.0292	0.018	0.0297	0.95	1.75	0.014
	(1.56)	(0.0029)	(1.63)	(0.0042)	(0.0104)	(0.168)				
BL	10.90	0.0217	11.29	−0.0058	0.0208	−0.159	0.0179	0.99	2.05	0.009
	(2.13)	(0.0042)	(2.20)	(0.0024)	(0.0079)	(0.227)				
BS	7.11	0.0104	6.88	0.0214	—	0.271	—	0.82	2.36	0.024
	(1.60)	(0.0032)	(1.62)	(0.0063)	—	(0.165)				
JU	7.46	0.0169	7.95	−0.0222	0.0188	0.184	0.0230	0.90	1.62	0.022
	(2.48)	(0.0047)	(2.63)	(0.0087)	(0.0220)	(0.271)				
SG	5.89	0.0136	6.06	−0.0010	0.0164	0.364	0.0258	0.98	1.68	0.011
	(1.19)	(0.0027)	(1.24)	(0.0030)	(0.0082)	(0.129)				
SO	7.95	0.0173	8.32	−0.0126	0.0198	0.144	0.0231	0.83	1.52	0.033
	(2.23)	(0.0052)	(2.43)	(0.0122)	(0.0230)	(0.239)				
TG	7.60	0.0159	7.90	−0.0085	0.0135	0.181	0.0165	0.94	2.14	0.018
	(1.80)	(0.0048)	(1.90)	(0.0055)	(0.0146)	(0.194)				
VS	6.85	0.0159	7.45	−0.0287	0.0083	0.250	0.0111	0.91	1.97	0.023
	(1.70)	(0.0031)	(1.83)	(0.0087)	(0.0207)	(0.185)				

H_0: $\beta_{BE,5} = \beta_{BL,5} = \beta_{JU,5} = \beta_{SG,5} = \beta_{SO,5} = \beta_{TG,5} = \beta_{VS,5}$
$\beta_{BE,6} = \beta_{BS,6} = \beta_{BL,6} = \beta_{JU,6} = \beta_{SG,6} = \beta_{SO,6} = \beta_{TG,6} = \beta_{VS,6}$

$X^2_{13} = 12.3$

y_{it} : log national income in canton i (real per capita)

C_{7890}, T_{7890} : constant and trend for the period 1978–1990

C_{9195}, T_{9195} : constant and trend for the period 1991–1995

D_{AKGS} : dummy variable for the abolishment of the capital gains tax in canton i

$\dfrac{\beta_{i5}}{1-\beta_{i6}}$: long-run level effect of the abolishment of the capital gains tax on national income

Standard errors in parentheses

Table 2: Effect of capital gains tax on real national income, 1978–1995: Restricted estimates

$$y_{it} = \beta_{i1}C_{7890} + \beta_{i2}T_{7890} + \beta_{i3}C_{9195} + \beta_{i4}T_{9195} + \beta_5 D_{AKGS} + \beta_6 y_{i, t-1}$$

/	β_{i1}	β_{i2}	β_{i3}	β_{i4}	β_{i5}	β_{i6}	$\dfrac{\beta_{i5}}{1-\beta_{i6}}$	$\overline{R}^2$	D.W.	SEE
BE	6.56	0.0096	6.72	−0.0045				0.95	2.02	0.013
	(0.63)	(0.0014)	(0.66)	(0.0035)						
BL	6.62	0.0124	6.85	−0.0046				0.98	2.51	0.011
	(0.63)	(0.0015)	(0.65)	(0.0027)						
BS	6.86	0.0100	6.62	0.0212				0.82	2.39	0.024
	(0.65)	(0.0020)	(0.67)	(0.0063)						
JU	6.43	0.0148	6.85	−0.0194				0.89	1.80	0.023
	(0.62)	(0.0020)	(0.66)	(0.0059)	0.0224	0.297	0.0319			
SG	6.51	0.0146	6.70	−0.0015	(0.0043)	(0.067)		0.98	1.76	0.012
	(0.62)	(0.0016)	(0.65)	(0.0030)						
SO	6.54	0.0141	6.77	−0.0067				0.84	1.72	0.032
	(0.63)	(0.0025)	(0.69)	(0.0086)						
TG	6.53	0.0125	6.76	−0.0068				0.94	2.31	0.019
	(0.62)	(0.0019)	(0.66)	(0.0049)						
VS	6.43	0.0136	6.97	−0.0270				0.92	2.36	0.022
	(0.62)	(0.0019)	(0.67)	(0.0062)						

y_{it} : log national income in canton i (real per capita)

C_{7890}, T_{7890} : constant and trend for the period 1978–1990

C_{9195}, T_{9195} : constant and trend for the period 1991–1995

D_{AKGS} : dummy variable for the abolishment of the capital gains tax in canton i

$\dfrac{\beta_{i5}}{1-\beta_{i6}}$: long-run level effect of the abolishment of the capital gains tax on national income

Standard errors in parentheses

within the few years after the abolishment of the tax for which data exist. However, in the long run even a very small increase in the growth rate would be much more important than the level effect we detected with the data available.

Our estimates of the effect on real income levels caused by abolishing capital gains taxation is subject to the following criticisms. First, the abolishment of the capital gains tax did not create new income but only shifted income from cantons with such taxes to cantons without them. Second, dummy variables only catch the strong economic growth in Switzerland in the second half of the 1980s.

To check the validity of these arguments, we estimated our trend model for the income for the remaining 18 cantons with the dummy variable starting in 1986. The results of this exercise are reported in table 3. As can be seen, the coefficient of the dummy variable of interest is statistically insignificant. This result implies that the cantons that retained capital gains taxes experienced neither a reduction nor an increase in real income. This finding clearly supports our main conclusion that abolishing the capital gains tax has a positive effect on the level of income.

Table 3: Effect of capital gains tax on real national income, 1978–1995: Dummy for boom years after 1986

$$y_t = \beta_1 C_{7890} + \beta_2 T_{7890} + \beta_3 C_{9195} + \beta_4 T_{9195} + \beta_5 D_{1987} + \beta_6 y_{t-1}$$

β_{i1}	β_{i2}	β_{i3}	β_{i4}	β_{i5}	β_{i6}	$\frac{\beta_{i5}}{1-\beta_{i6}}$	R^2	D.W.	SEE
3.53	0.0096	3.63	−0.0016	0.0094	0.626	0.0251			
(2.49)	(0.0053)	(2.64)	(0.0061)	(0.0172)	(0.265)		0.98	2.12	0.012

y_{it} : log national income in 18 cantons without abolishment of capital gains tax (real per capita)

C_{7890}, T_{7890} : constant and trend for the period 1978–1990

C_{9195}, T_{9195} : constant and trend for the period 1991–1995

D_{AKGS}: dummy variable for the abolishment of the capital gains tax in canton i

$\frac{\beta_{i5}}{1-\beta_{i6}}$: long-run level effect of the abolishment of the capital gains tax on national income

Standard errors in parentheses

A third objection to our main findings is that the abolishment of capital gains taxation is just one of many new measures introduced by newly elected liberal cantonal governments. However, this was not true in the eight cantons considered. As in all Swiss cantons, governments in these eight were formed through coalitions with directly elected members. Such coalitions tend to develop economic policies smoothly rather than through sudden, major changes. In addition, there is evidence that capital gains taxation was abolished because it was considered to be a tax that produced low revenues and required high administrative costs.

Effects on tax revenue

Second, we estimated a trend model for real direct tax revenue in the eight cantons. The basic hypothesis is that the elimination of the capital gains tax results in lower tax revenues for the relevant cantons. Following the approach developed in the study of income, we obtained the results reported in table 4 in the test of this hypothesis. As can be seen, abolishing the capital gains tax has had no statistically negative effect on real tax revenues. This result is due to the fact that the increases in real income caused by abolishing the tax caused a corresponding increase in other tax revenues, which replaced those lost through abolishing the capital gains tax.

The revenue of the capital gains tax: Empirical results for Basel-Stadt

Proponents for the imposition of a capital gains tax at the federal level in Switzerland support their arguments by optimistic forecasts of the revenues generated by such a tax. These forecasts are calculated simply by multiplying the increase in the value of outstanding stocks by the tax rate proposed. Such estimates are biased upward for two main reasons. First, a significant proportion of all stocks is owned by companies and is, therefore, already subject to profit taxation. Second, the realization of stock-market capital gains is at the discretion of households.

To study the effects of a capital gains tax on revenues, it is necessary to have separate revenue data of this tax. Such data do not exist for most cantons, but they are available for Basel-Stadt for the

Table 4: Effect of capital gains tax on real tax revenue, 1978–1995

$$s_{it} = \beta_{i1}C_{7890} + \beta_{i2}T_{7890} + \beta_{i3}C_{9195} + \beta_{i4}T_{9195} + \beta_{i5}D_{AKGS} + \beta_{i6}so_{i,t-1}$$

i	β_{i1}	β_{i2}	β_{i3}	β_{i4}	β_{i5}	β_{i6}	$\dfrac{\beta_{i5}}{1-\beta_{i6}}$	$\overline{R}^2$	D.W.	SEE
BE	8.12	0.0186	8.19	0.0123	−0.0258	−0.238	−0.0426	0.60	1.85	0.037
	(0.97)	(0.0038)	(0.97)	(0.0094)	(0.0264)	(0.147)				
BL	8.39	0.0151	8.22	0.0206	0.0947	−0.230	0.0770	0.84	1.79	0.032
	(0.71)	(0.0032)	(0.73)	(0.0082)	(0.0215)	(0.104)				
BS	4.90	0.0173	5.06	0.0021	—	0.363	—	0.82	1.27	0.042
	(1.08)	(0.0042)	(1.11)	(0.0107)	—	(0.140)				
JU	10.65	0.0279	11.32	−0.0214	−0.0307	−0.682	−0.0183	0.70	1.81	0.029
	(1.22)	(0.0042)	(1.34)	(0.0081)	(0.0226)	(0.194)				
SG	5.58	0.0324	5.47	0.0321	−0.0073	0.099	−0.0081	0.90	1.66	0.044
	(0.76)	(0.0048)	(0.81)	(0.0111)	(0.0304)	(0.122)				
SO	10.69	0.0221	11.62	−0.0420	0.1619	−0.680	0.0964	0.87	2.76	0.036
	(0.85)	(0.0035)	(0.93)	(0.0096)	(0.0290)	(0.134)				
TG	6.60	0.0193	6.82	−0.0035	0.0185	−0.036	0.0179	0.84	2.55	0.027
	(1.04)	(0.0038)	(1.12)	(0.0073)	(0.0199)	(0.163)				
VS	4.15	0.0013	4.33	−0.0144	0.0425	0.363	0.0667	0.35	2.29	0.042
	(1.38)	(0.0054)	(1.56)	(0.0132)	(0.0348)	(0.214)				

y_{it} : log total direct tax revenue in canton i (real per capita)

C_{7890}, T_{7890} : constant and trend for the period 1978–1990

C_{9195}, T_{9195} : constant and trend for the period 1991–1995

D_{AKGS}: dummy variable for the abolishment of the capital gains tax in canton i

$\dfrac{\beta_{i5}}{1-\beta_{i6}}$: long-run level effect of the abolishment of the capital gains tax on national income

Standard errors in parentheses

years from 1965 to 1995, covering revenue estimates from the capital gains tax on movable and non-movable property. We used these data to study the revenues from the capital gains tax on movable property in Basel-Stadt in the hope of shedding light on the likely revenues from imposing such a tax at the federal level.

The simplest approach to estimating the revenue potential of the tax on movable property consists of subtracting the mean value of the period from 1990 to 1995 (with the tax on all property) from the mean for the period from 1965 to 1989 (with the tax on non-movable property only). However, this approach results in an inefficient estimate since tax revenue measured as a share of business and property income is strongly autocorrelated. We account for this correlation by estimating an autoregressive model for the revenue indicator from the capital gains tax. We used a dummy variable which takes the value 1 for the years 1990 to 1995 and is 0 before 1990 to represent the change in mean by the abolishment of the tax on movable property in 1990. The first panel of table 5 shows the estimation results for this model. The AR(1) coefficient estimate (0.73) indicates a high persistence of the capital gains tax revenue indicator. The intercept term estimate (1.25) means that the long-run mean of the revenue is slightly above 1% before the abolishment of the tax on movable property. The coefficient estimate of the dummy variable (–0.99) indicates that abolishing the tax in 1990 led to a long-run reduction of the tax revenue by nearly 1%. Therefore, the revenue potential of a capital gains tax on movable property is approximately 1% of business and property income according to the data for Basel-Stadt. If we apply this share to total Swiss business and property income, we arrive at a revenue potential of around 700 million Francs, which is only one fifth of the revenue forecasts put forward by the proponents of a capital gains tax.

It could be argued this estimate is biased downwards as the data analyzed do not reflect the stock-market boom of the 1990s and a perhaps permanently higher growth-rate of stock-market prices. In order to check this argument, it is important to know how realized capital gains are influenced by the development of stock-market prices. On the one hand, capital-gains realizations may be a function of the average growth rate of stock prices. On the other hand, realizations may be a function of gains due to price increases above the longer-run trend.

Table 5: Capital gains tax revenue, business and property income in Basel Stadt and stock market prices

$$\left(\frac{KGS}{VE}\right)_t = (1-\beta_3)\beta_1 + \beta_2(D_{AKGS(-1)} - \beta_3 D_{AKGSt-2}) + \beta_3\left(\frac{KGS}{VE}\right)_{t-1}$$

β_1	β_2	β_3	$\overline{R}^2$	D.W.	SEE
1.25	−0.99	0.73	0.67	1.77	0.29
(0.21)	(0.29)	(0.13)			

$$\left(\frac{KGS}{VE}\right)_t = \beta_1 + \beta_2 \Delta AI_{t-1} + \beta_3\left(\frac{KGS}{VE}\right)_{t-1}$$

β_1	β_2	β_3	$\overline{R}^2$	D.W.	SEE
0.132	0.00684	0.875	0.58	1.78	0.29
(0.199)	(0.00294)	(0.150)			

$$\left(\frac{KGS}{VE}\right)_t = \beta_1 + \beta_2 DTAI_{t-1} + \beta_3\left(\frac{KGS}{VE}\right)_{t-1}$$

β_1	β_2	β_3	$\overline{R}^2$	D.W.	SEE
0.512	0.00944	0.596	0.78	2.34	0.22
(0.133)	(0.00176)	(0.100)			

$$\left(\frac{KGS}{VE}\right)_t = \beta_1 + \beta_2 DTAI_{t-1} + \beta_3(\Delta AI_{t-1} - \beta_4 \Delta AI_{t-2}) + \beta_4\left(\frac{KGS}{VE}\right)_{t-1}$$

β_1	β_2	β_3	β_4	$\overline{R}^2$	D.W.	SEE
0.611	0.0106	−0.0018	0.514	0.78	2.22	0.21
(0.183)	(0.0024)	(0.0029)	(0.138)			

$\left(\frac{KGS}{VE}\right)_t$: Capital gains tax revenue/business and property income canton Basel-Stadt

D_{AKGS}: Dummy variable, from 1990 onwards = 1

ΔAI_t, $DTAI_t$ v: Growth rate of real Swiss stock prices and deviation from linear trend, respectively

Standard errors in parentheses

To test these competing hypotheses, we estimate a dynamic model for our capital gains tax-revenue variable. Besides the lagged endogenous variable in the first variant, the lagged growth rate of real Swiss stock prices is included. In the second model, this variable is replaced by the lagged deviation from a log linear trend. The lag reflects the fact that taxes have to be paid with a one-year lag in Basel-Stadt. The results reported in the second, third and fourth panel of table 5 show clearly that the trend-deviation specification performs better than the growth-rate specification. Thus, linking the expected return of a capital gains tax to the growth of stock prices may be very misleading.

Conclusions

In 1996, the capital gains tax on movable property, like shares, was abolished completely at the cantonal level in Switzerland. The strong increase in stock market prices in the second half of the 1990s led to an initiative referendum to reintroduce such a tax at the confederation level in 1999. However, general economic reasoning on the features of the Swiss tax system and empirical evidence from cantonal data provide strong arguments against the introduction of such a tax.

First, the effective tax burden on capital in Switzerland already is relatively high compared to that of other countries and compared to that on consumption. In particular, the difference between the effective tax burden on labour and capital is relatively low by international standards. Moreover, an empirical analysis of the abolishment of the capital gains tax on movable property in eight cantons in the period from 1986 to 1990, shows that this measure increased the level of real cantonal income and did not reduce overall tax revenues. An additional argument against the imposition of a capital gains tax is that all capital gains on movable capital, whether they are realized or not, are already taxed implicitly through cantonal wealth taxes.

Second, the introduction of the proposed capital gains tax would lead to inefficiencies through induced changes in the behaviour of households and companies aimed at the avoidance of the tax. In addition, the proposed tax would increase the already high administrative costs of the very complex Swiss tax system. These additional costs are likely to be high relative to the expected low revenues from the additional tax. We expect the federal tax on movable capital gains to be much smaller than is suggested by the advocates of the tax. Our expectations are based on an empirical analysis of the tax revenue generated by the capital gains tax in the canton Basel-Stadt in the years from 1965 to 1990. We found that in this canton the capital gains tax raised revenues of only 1% of business and property income. This result is easy to understand, as we know that, in reaction to such a tax, there will be locking in and locking out of capital gains by households and companies. Thus, inefficiencies in private financial behaviour and low tax revenues are the result of such a tax. In addition, we found that realizations tend to be made only on temporary deviations from the trend and not the level of stock-market prices, so that revenue estimates based on recent average prices are seriously biased upward.

Notes

1 These figures are calculated using the method developed by Mendoza, Razin and Tesar (1994)
2 For the details the reader is referred to Federal Tax Administration (1999).
3 Income taxes are clearly higher in the French-speaking cantons .
4 Community income taxes are linked directly to cantonal income taxes; they are paid as a percentage of canton taxes, which varies from community to community.
5 Some references on the taxation of capital are Atkinson and Sandmo (1980), Chamley (1986), Jones, Manuelli and Rossi (1997), Razin and Sadka (1989). Some special references with respect to capital gains taxation are Auerbach (1989) and Poterba (1987, 1989).
6 Years when capital gains tax was abolished: BE 1987, BL 1987, BS 1990, JU 1989, SG 1987, SO 1986, TG 1987 und VS 1987.
7 Of course, alternatively we could adopt the hypothesis of difference stationary series. However, if we calculate the Dickey-Fuller Statistic with the AR(1) coefficient estimate in table 2, we obtain a value of –10.5, which is very large in absolute value and, therefore, at odds with the difference stationarity hypothesis, even if we account that our SUR estimate with broken trend does not correspond to the standard Dickey-Fuller framework.
8 We excluded the estimate for the canton Basel-Stadt since the break in the trend function coincides with the abolishment of the capital gains tax in 1990.
9 The level effect is consistent with the Solow growth model whereas, in new or endogenous growth models, a growth-rate effect is to occur.

References

Atkinson, A.B., and A. Sandmo (1980). Welfare Implications of the Taxation of Savings. *Economic Journal* 90: 529–49.

Auerbach, A.J. (1989). Capital Gains Taxation and Tax Reform. *National Tax Journal*, 42, 3: 391–401.

Chamley, C.P. (1986). Optimal Taxation of Capital Income in General Equilibrium with Infinite Lives. *Econometrica* 54: 607–22.

Cnossen, S. (1997). Dual Income Taxation: The Nordic Experience. *Research Memorandum 9710*. Rotterdam: Erasmus University Rotterdam.

Duss, R., and R. Bird (1979). Switzerland's Tax Jungle. *Canadian Tax Journal* 1, 27: 46-67.

Federal Tax Administration (1999). *Federal, Cantonal and Communal Taxes: An Outline of the Swiss Tax System*. Bern: Federal Tax Administration.

Grubel, Herbert (2000). *Unlocking Canadian Capital: The Case for Capital Gains Tax Reform*. Vancouver, BC: The Fraser Institute.

Jaeger, A., K. Hviding, and C. Purfield (1999). *International Monetary Fund: Switzerland-Selected Issues and Statistical Appendix*. Washington, DC: International Monetary Fund.

Jones, L.E., R.E. Manuelli, and P.E. Rossi (1997). On the Optional Taxation of Capital Income. *Journal of Economic Theory* 73: 93–117.

Lucas, R.E. (1990). Supply-Side Economics: An Analytical Review. *Oxford Economic Papers* 42: 293–316.

Mendoza, E., A. Razin, and L. Tesar (1994). Effective Tax Rates in Macroeconomics Cross-Country Estimates of Tax Rates on Factor Income and Consumption. *Journal of Monetary Economics* 34: 297–323.

Poterba, J.M. (1987). Are Capital Gains Taxed? Evidence from the United States. *Journal of Public Economics* 33, 2: 157–72.

——— (1989). Capital Gains Tax Policy toward Entrepreneurship. *National Tax Journal* 42, 3: 375–89.

Razin, A., and E. Sadka (1989). *International Tax Competition and Gains from Tax Harmonization*. Working Paper No. 3152. Cambridge, MA: National Bureau of Economic Research.

Stiglitz, J.E. (1983). Some Aspects of the Taxation of Capital Gains. *Journal of Public Economics* 21, 2: 257–94.

Capital gains tax
The New Zealand case

Robin Oliver

New Zealand does not have a general capital gains tax, nor does it levy tax on inheritances. This makes New Zealand unusual among member countries of the OECD. We inherited our lack of capital gains taxation, along with most of our other legal and constitutional framework, from the English. But, in contrast with other countries (the United States, United Kingdom, Canada, and Australia) with a similar inheritance, we have retained an income tax that does not include capital gains in the taxation base. This paper, therefore, uses New Zealand as a sort of case study of what life is like when capital gains are not taxed. I comment on this from my personal perspective, which is that of someone who was a tax practitioner and is now a tax enforcer and a tax-policy adviser.

As a general rule, capital gains in New Zealand are not income for the purposes of our income-tax system. Indeed, our courts have held that our income tax law does not even recognize the concept of capital gains. In our law, capital gains are not exempt or untaxed

---

The views expressed in this paper are those of the author and not necessarily those of the New Zealand Inland Revenue Department or of the New Zealand Government. Note will be found on page 87.

income; they have no legal recognition. This means, for example, that there is no requirement to apportion interest expenses to the derivation of taxed income and untaxed capital gains.

Nevertheless, our income tax legislation (the Income Tax Act 1994) includes in taxable "income" many forms of gain that, in the absence of specific legislation, would generally be considered capital gains. Each such provision has its own history. Very broadly, since the income tax was first introduced in New Zealand in 1891, our Parliament has considered it necessary to prevent people from characterizing otherwise taxable income as untaxed capital gain. The result is detailed and often complex legislation, as described below.

The tax regime in New Zealand is not easily classified. On one hand, we have no explicit capital gains tax. On the other hand, we include in taxable income many items that, in other jurisdictions, would be treated as capital gains. In other words, New Zealand does not have an explicit capital gains tax but taxes some capital gains as conventionally defined.

In my view, New Zealand's treatment of capital gains is due to the fact that any income-tax system that leaves all capital gains tax-free is essentially unworkable. On the other hand, I am not aware of any income tax system that taxes all capital gains under all circumstances. The issue, therefore, is the extent to which capital gains are taxed. Different countries have positioned themselves at different points along a spectrum from fully untaxed to fully taxed. New Zealand is near the untaxed end of the spectrum. However, the spectrum is not one-dimensional. Depending on the type of assets under consideration, New Zealand can be located near the fully taxed end of the spectrum. Debt instruments and certain overseas equity holdings of residents are examples of these asset types. In these cases, New Zealand's legislation can tax all capital gains on a full accrual basis.

Bearing these points in mind, this paper focuses on the effects of a tax system that does not tax capital gains explicitly. One of the most important conclusions to be reached is that conditions in New Zealand totally refute Professor Herbert Grubel's claim that: "If the capital gains tax were abandoned completely, many government employees, and private sector tax accountants and lawyers could be re-employed to produce goods and services valued by society more than the enforcement and manipulation of the tax code" (Grubel 2000: 30).

As an experienced accountant and lawyer, I have found that, even in the absence of a capital gains tax, many people are employed both in manipulating and enforcing tax legislation. Often the main job of these people is specifically to deal with problems of defining and enforcing the border between taxed income and untaxed gains that is due to the very absence of the capital gains tax.

Simplicity has not been the outcome of a lack of capital gains tax in New Zealand. Nor, is there much evidence to suggest that the absence of taxes on capital gains has had a marked effect on investment, capital markets, and overall economic performance. A possible but unlikely exception here is the propensity for New Zealanders to hold their wealth in the form of real property. From my perspective, the most marked effect of not having a specific capital gains tax has been to introduce a host of inconsistencies and complexities into our income-tax rules.

In the remainder of this paper I will focus on the way in which the absence of capital gains taxes has created incentives to change behaviour in order to reduce overall tax obligations. I will also discuss how efforts of the government to reduce such incentives have resulted in illogical and inconsistent policies, which turn out to be resistant to improvement.

Personally, I am neither for nor against a capital gains tax in New Zealand. The issue requires a detailed weighing up of arguments for and against such a tax. However, as my analysis will show, for those who oppose all capital gains taxation, New Zealand's experiences illustrate that the grass is not always greener on the other side of the fence.

New Zealand income-tax law

New Zealand has two main forms of taxation, the income tax and the Goods and Services Tax (a VAT). The income tax is levied uniformly on all personal, business, and investment income. There is no separate set of tax rules for the corporate or any other sector.

New Zealand's income tax legislation leaves the term "income" undefined. The judiciary has instead provided the operational definition of income. The judiciary turned to trust law and other precedents for the definition of income. In general, this meant that most increases in the value of assets, other than trading stock, were excluded from the tax base. This outcome relied on concepts from trust law that differentiated the interests of the life tenant (entitled to income) from the interests of the remainder man (entitled to capital and so to the realization of capital assets of the trust).

Our assertion that New Zealand has no capital gains taxation rests on these principles of trust law. It is obvious that the trust law is devoid of economic concepts and principles. As the New Zealand Royal Commission on Social Policy commented: "With hindsight it seems surprising that concepts of trust law were considered an appropriate substitute for a direct focus on economic efficiency and equity concerns in the raising of taxes" (New Zealand Royal Commission on Social Policy 1988: 450).

In practice, it is difficult to distinguish between income and assets. The Privy Council noted in *BP Australia Limited* v *FCT* that the distinction is "sometimes difficult to draw and leads to distinctions of some subtlety between profit that is made 'out of' assets and profit that is made 'upon' assets or 'with' assets" ([1964] AC 244 at 262).

An example of this difficulty can be found in the area of investment and financial intermediation. Thus, a mutual fund managing a portfolio of shares is usually taxed on profits from the sale of shares in its portfolio. The rationale for this interpretation is that the selling of shares is a normal part of the business of such an entity. A small investor holding shares directly, on the other hand, is not taxed on capital gains realized through the sale of shares. However, these general rules have been modified through rulings by New Zealand's Inland Revenue Department in relation to the operation of index funds. The Department has ruled that an index fund does not hold shares on revenue account and can make tax-free capital gains, mainly because its share purchases and sales are not part of a business but determined by the requirements of the index. This ruling provides a tax incentive for investments in passive rather than actively managed funds.

The poorly defined boundary between income and capital provides many opportunities for tax advisers and many problems for the revenue authority. In the case of trusts, the courts have decided that the increase in trust assets can be classified as income or capital according to the intention of the person who originally transferred assets to the trust. It is obvious that, in general, taxpayers will attempt to define profits as capital gains and consider all expenses deductible from profit producing revenues. For this reason, the tax authorities have been faced with the need to define as taxable income many items that would otherwise have been tax-free capital gains.

The following are some examples of how New Zealand has legislatively broadened what is included in taxable income.

Gains from the sale of personal property

The legislation taxes profits or gains from the sale of property where the taxpayer is a dealer in such property. Interpreted literally, this legislation would apply even where the property on which the profit was made was held for purposes other than dealing. However, the courts have restricted the provision to assets held for trading purposes. Thus, the provision does not make taxable what would normally be considered to be capital gains.

Legislation also makes taxable all profits or gains from the sale of property acquired for the purpose of sale. This means that shares acquired for their dividend yield give rise to untaxed gains, while those acquired for their capital yield do not. In practice, this distinction has given rise to lengthy case law, which sets out more precisely under what conditions property is considered to be acquired with the purpose of sale and, therefore, taxable; and under which it is acquired without the intention of sale and, therefore, not taxable.

Legislation has also made gains from profit-making undertakings or schemes taxable. However, the courts have interpreted this provision so strictly that it does not tax anything that would otherwise be considered a capital gain.

Land transactions

New Zealand income-tax legislation has detailed and complex provisions bringing many gains on land transactions into the tax net. This legislation was designed to counter the situation whereby land developers and builders claimed all of their income to be non-taxable capital gains so that developers and builders became in effect untaxed occupations. In broad terms, New Zealand taxes gains on the sale of land acquired with an intention of resale by land dealers, developers, and builders, including gains due to the rezoning, subdivision, or development of land. There are exceptions to these rules for private residences, business premises, and farmland.

Income from debt instruments

The difficulty of sustaining the traditional distinction between profits and capital gains is particularly acute with respect to debt instruments. If lenders can make a return that is taxable by way of coupon payments or tax-free by way of a redemption payment, they will always prefer the latter. In the United Kingdom, realized profits on discounts of financial instruments were made taxable profits as early as 1805. Since 1986, New Zealand has gone further and put a similar law in place, which taxes all gains from the holding of debt instruments as they accrue.

Foreign investment fund rules

New Zealand aims to tax the worldwide income of its residents, including income derived by offshore companies and similar entities. Since it is not possible to subject foreign entities to a national tax, New Zealand levies an accrued capital gains tax on all foreign portfolio equity investments. This rule does not apply to companies resident in Australia, Canada, Germany, Japan, Norway, the United Kingdom, and the United States. Non-portfolio gains are subject to controlled foreign company rules. These require the shareholders of subsidiaries to return as income their proportion of the profits of those foreign subsidiaries. The profits of foreign subsidiaries are calculated in accordance with normal New Zealand tax laws so that, for non-portfolio investments, capital gains remain tax-free.

The results

It is difficult to know what effect New Zealand's lack of a capital gains tax has had on her capital markets. The New Zealand stock exchange has not been noted for its high performance in recent years with a price index still below the high it achieved in October 1987. It is also worth noting that New Zealand's listed share prices are strongly influenced by non-resident investors who hold up to 40% of the value of total market capitalization. Such shareholders have been the marginal investors and, while they have played an important role in the determination of share prices, they tend not to be affected by not having to pay New Zealand's capital gains taxes. That is because, even if New Zealand had a capital gains tax, in most cases foreign investors would not be subject to such a tax under New Zealand's double-tax agreements.

There is also little evidence that the absence of capital gains taxes has encouraged entrepreneurial endeavours in New Zealand. The country's business expenditure on research and development and its post-war economic performance have been well below the OECD average. In 1997/1998, our business expenditure on research and development was 0.32% compared with an OECD average of 1.48% of GDP.

It is not clear what role New Zealand's tax system plays in the pattern of asset holdings by households. Direct equity is most favoured by the tax system yet it constitutes a very small proportion of household assets. Debt instruments and equity held through intermediaries are not tax-favoured to the same extent but constitute a much higher proportion of wealth. Average annual real capital gains on housing since 1960 have been around 1% while untaxed, imputed, annual real increases in housing income amounted to about 2% to 2.5%. The practice of not taxing imputed rental income is a feature of most tax systems and in New Zealand it is significantly clawed back by not allowing the deduction of mortgage interest.

For many years until the later 1980s, New Zealand experienced high rates of inflation, paid government subsidies on many investments, and controlled interest rates, which often were negative in real terms. It is likely that these conditions have played a greater role in setting the pattern of private investment than did the tax system. Similarly, the country's economic growth rates have probably been influenced more by inflation and other government policies than by the absence of a capital gains tax.

It has been argued that the absence of a capital gains tax creates a strong incentive for the excessive reinvestment of business profits, which erodes the tax base and causes the inefficient withholding of funds from potentially higher yields in other employment. There is no evidence that such excessive reinvestment of profits has taken place in New Zealand in spite of the absence of a capital gains tax. The average dividend yield of New Zealand's listed companies is about 5% to 7% annually, which is high by world standards. That high yield indicates that the lack of capital gain taxation does not lead to excessive corporate reinvestment. Smaller companies tend to distribute most of their available income to the owners.

The reasons for these high-dividend returns on business investment are likely to lie in the overall structure of the tax system, in particular, the fact that salaries are deductible from the business income-tax base and dividends carry credits for taxes paid at the corporate level.[1] Until April 1, 2000, the company rate was at 33% and equal to the top personal marginal tax rate so that there were no incentives to retain profits. In fact, because personal income-tax rates are progressive, a positive incentive exists to distribute rather than retain income whenever the effective personal income-tax rate is less than the corporate income-tax rate.

From April 1, 2000, New Zealand's top personal marginal tax rate was increased from 33% to 39%. The company and trustee tax rates remained at 33%. It is likely that this will lead to increased retention of profits. That will be balanced by the increased advantage from income splitting by making distributions to family members with low tax rates.

In general, however, it is the overall nature of the tax system, such as the rate structure and the manner in which dividends are taxed, that can lead the tax system to encourage excessive profit retention. The presence or absence of a capital gains tax seems peripheral.

Problems created by not taxing capital gains

The conclusion of the previous section was that the absence of a capital gains tax has not had an easily identifiable impact on the economy. Earlier, however, I described some of the complexities of New Zealand's income-tax legislation caused by not taxing capital gains. Why the legislative complexity in the absence of discernible impacts?

The main reason for the complexity of the tax laws is that the absence of a capital gains tax reduces the income-tax base and results in the following consequences. First, artificial boundaries are required between what is taxable and what is not taxable. Defining those boundaries leads to complex tax legislation. It also leads to policy inconsistencies and unintended incentives built into the tax structure. These problems cannot be resolved without moving closer to a concept of economic income and the consequent removal of the distinction between capital and the revenue it produces. Secondly, working on these distinctions is the life-blood of tax planners and a prime hunting ground for tax-planning schemes. The remainder of this paper considers these two issues by way of examples drawn from the New Zealand experience.

Structural problems created by the distinction
between capital and income

The problems created by the need to distinguish between capital and income from capital can best be illustrated by the inconsistent tax rules affecting individuals' choices of investment in shares or bonds. This choice can be made directly or indirectly through an intermediary such as a mutual fund. The lack of a general capital gains tax has resulted in a series of rules that generally encourage direct over indirect investment and equity over debt instruments.

First, dividends are taxable as ordinary income. The problem of double taxation of corporate income is overcome by allowing the dividend recipient to get a credit for tax paid at the corporate level. However, when a company distributes to its shareholders a capital gain, no tax credit is available because no company tax has been paid. The end result is that the capital gains exemption provided at the company level is clawed back when the gain is distributed as a dividend. If, on the other hand, the shareholder holds equities directly and not through an intermediary company, the shareholder retains the benefit of tax-free capital gains.

Trusts are not subject to this dividend claw-back, so an investment made through a trust retains the benefit of tax-free capital gains. That clearly places trusts at an advantage over companies as an investment intermediary. In response, New Zealand legislation deems certain trusts to be companies subject to the dividend rules, which prevent the tax-free realization of capital gains to its owners. Trusts treated in this way solicit investments much as mutual funds do in North America. Although this particular treatment of trusts shores up the tax base, it creates a bias against the use of trusts and the financial intermediation they provide.

The same incentive against financial intermediation is created by the general common-law rule that profits from the sale of shares held in a managed portfolio are taxable as ordinary business income. This rule makes it impossible for most intermediaries to make capital gains even if they can distribute the profits tax free.

As noted above, capital gains made by index funds are not subject to the same rule. They are considered not to be trading shares and, therefore, capital gains are not seen to be arising from a taxable trading activity. It is clear that this special treatment of index funds creates incentives for investors to invest in them rather actively managed or ordinary passively managed funds. Such incentives cause economic inefficiencies and therefore are undesirable.

As a government policy adviser, I can say that there was never a deliberate intention to design a set of tax rules that exhibit the biases just noted: the discouragement of intermediation and the encouragement of passively over actively managed equity portfolios. These rules have arisen from the need to protect a tax base that is eroded by the failure to tax capital gains.

A second example of a problem caused by the lack of a capital gains tax involves share repurchases by the issuing company. Conceptually, a share repurchase is equivalent to the distribution of a dividend by a firm because both methods result in the transfer of corporate assets to shareholders. However, dividend payments are taxable while the capital gains realized through the repurchase of shares are not. This asymmetric tax treatment of company reserves distributed to shareholders introduces incentives to favour share repurchase over the distribution of dividends. Other countries deal with this issue by taxing share repurchases either as a dividend or as a capital gain. New Zealand does not have that option and had to adopt complex rules and somewhat arcane legislation. Under these rules, some taxpayers are taxed on gains they have not made, while others are not taxed on gains they have made.

Depreciation creates a further problem for New Zealand's tax system because it has no capital gains tax. It is well known that the depreciation of assets imposes an often unrealized decline in wealth on its owners and implicitly on the net income earned from the asset during the relevant period. Since New Zealand's income-tax system was based on the non-recognition of changes in asset values, the original income-tax system did not provide for the depreciation of assets in the calculation of tax obligations. However, soon after the initial legislation was passed, it was realized that the absence of depreciation allowances resulted in the over-taxation of business income. Consequently, Parliament corrected this mistake and passed legislation that allowed depreciation to be treated as a special allowance. Unfortunately, the use of depreciation as an allowance creates an asymmetry in a tax system that does not tax capital gains. Declines in asset values give rise to deductions while increases are tax-free.

Tax planning problems created by distinction
between capital and income from capital

The preceding section contained a number of examples of special rules in New Zealand's tax code that were adopted to deal with perverse incentives stemming from the absence of a capital gains tax. These rules give rise to many opportunities to plan financial affairs for the avoidance of taxes by attempting to get all accretions to wealth on tax-free capital account and all expenditure on deductible revenue account. There are many, ingenious methods to achieve this; the following are a few examples.

The average salary earner has few opportunities to earn tax-free capital sums. One opportunity is a redundancy payment received upon losing a job. Traditionally, such a payment was considered a tax-free capital payment to the employee. Since in many circumstances such payments could be traded off for taxable salary, the New Zealand Parliament made redundancy payments taxable. However, payments for humiliation on redundancy have retained their tax-free status. As this opportunity has become more widely known, New Zealand employers have shown a tendency to ensure that redundant staff have been subject to increasing levels of humiliation.

In a similar way, employers have shown an increasing tendency to provide workers with capital payments to induce them to leave their previous occupations or to accept restrictive covenants, which limit their ability to work elsewhere. Courts have decided that such payments are not taxable. The apparent ability to substitute in this way tax-free for otherwise taxable remuneration has led the Government recently to introduce legislation to prevent these practices.

Another example of a practice that turns taxable income into non-taxable capital gains involved an international accounting firm, which received a lump-sum payment in return for leasing for very high rental payments floors of a commercial building. The receipt of the up-front lump sum offset the high annual rental payments so that in present value terms the net effect was a lease cut at prevailing market levels. The Privy Council held that the lump-sum payment was a tax-free capital gain, even though the firm then received deductions for its above-market annual rental payments.

Another, even more imaginative method for turning taxable income into capital gains involves the fact that New Zealand levies tax on the worldwide income of residents, including that generated through offshore subsidiaries. To avoid this tax on foreign income a New Zealand company can pay an unrelated non-resident bank a sum of money. In return for this money, the company receives the option to purchase, for a minimal amount, shares in a New Zealand subsidiary of the non-resident bank created especially for this purpose. The bank then invests the sum tax-free in a haven and eventually invests the capital plus tax-free interest in its New Zealand subsidiary. The New Zealand company then sells the shares that give it ownership of the foreign bank subsidiary and makes a tax free-capital gain.

Another practice for tax avoidance is used by very wealthly individuals who borrow funds offshore. The funds are used to invest in a New Zealand company. The loan is "back-ended" so that no payments are required until the loan matures, although accrued interest on the borrowings is deductible. The New Zealand company expends the funds on a high-risk venture (in which the lender also has an interest), giving rise to further tax deductions. The loan plus interest is repaid at maturity as investors exercise an option to put their interest in the venture entity for the principal plus interest. The profit is a tax-free capital gain. The investor, for an up-front investment, receives a return by way of substantial tax deductions.

There are many other examples I could present to illustrate the sophisticated methods used by New Zealanders to turn income into capital gains. Suffice it to note that human ingenuity and the profit motive are likely to come up with new schemes, whatever efforts are made by the tax authorities to prevent the abuse. This dynamic process and the cost of monitoring it certainly are highly undesirable and inefficient consequences of a tax system that fails to tax capital gains.

Proposals for reform in New Zealand

The structural problems that the lack of tax on capital gains poses for our income tax system have not gone unnoticed. A number of reviews of the tax system have considered the extent to which New Zealand should tax such gains.

In 1966, the Government established a committee of independent experts (the Ross Committee) to undertake a comprehensive review of all aspects of central government taxation in New Zealand. The committee reported in October 1967 (Government of New Zealand 1967). It noted that there was a strong justification for taxing realized capital gains, although it considered the issue needed further study and any reforms in this area should follow implementation of other reforms such as lower marginal income-tax rates.

In 1982, a task force on tax reform reported (New Zealand Government 1982). It concluded that, although there was no reason in principle not to tax capital gains, it did not recommend the introduction of a capital gains tax at that time. The task force's views seemed to be influenced by its view that introducing a capital gains tax during a period of high inflation, as then prevailed, would create more problems than it would cure.

In 1989, the then Labour Government did propose the taxation of capital gains, along with across-the-board indexation of the income tax base (New Zealand Government 1989). With the defeat of that Government in a General Election late in that year, the proposals did not proceed.

In 1998, the then Government established a "Committee of Experts" to review a number of aspects of the tax system, including compliance costs and how to make the tax system more robust against avoidance. The committee reported in December 1998 (New Zealand Government 1998). Whether capital gains should be taxed was outside the Committee's terms of reference. The committee did comment, however, that the benefits of a capital gains tax would depend on the proposed package of taxation reform of which it was a part.

Finally, the Labour-Alliance Coalition Government formed at the end of 1999 has stated that it will not introduce a capital gains tax in its first term of office. The Government has announced an inquiry into the tax system. Questions that will be posed to the Inquiry include whether the tax system can be made fairer and whether the income-tax base should be broadened. This may involve consideration of the issues surrounding the taxation of capital gains.

Conclusion

This paper has canvassed the problems posed for New Zealand's tax system by the absence of a general capital gains tax. Undoubtedly, if we had a capital gains tax, the paper would have canvassed the problems posed by having such a tax. Certainly, designing an efficient capital gains tax raises a number of issues for policy makers. They include the following:

- whether the tax base needs to be indexed for inflation;
- whether gains should become taxable upon accrual or realization (or disposal)
- the range of capital gains to which the tax is to be applied, especially whether is should include private residences;
- the treatment of capital losses;
- the appropriate rate of tax.

The basic issue in practice is not whether or not, but the extent to which, capital gains should be taxed. The extent should be chosen after careful analysis of what optimizes fairness and efficiency, all within the context of each country's tax structure and system. There is probably no unique and perfect design for such a tax system.

However, I would assert, after my long experience with New Zealand's tax regime as a private consultant and government adviser that the best possible system is not one that simply excludes capital gains from taxable income. For practical, if not economic, reasons, nor would an optimal tax system be likely to include the full taxation of capital gains on an accruals basis.

Note

1 Small, family-owned companies can pay out dividends from income on which no company tax is payable (such as capital gains) tax-free under the qualifying company rules.

References

Grubel, H.G. (2000). *Unlocking Canadian Capital: The Case for Capital Gains Tax Reform*. Vancouver, BC: The Fraser Institute.

New Zealand Royal Commission on Social Policy (1988). *April 1988 Report 3, 2*. Wellington, NZ.

Government of New Zealand (1967). *The Report of the New Zealand Taxation Review Committee Chaired by Sir Lewis Ross*. Wellington, New Zealand.

New Zealand Government (1982). *The Report of the Task Force on Tax Reform Chaired by P.M. McCaw*. Wellington, New Zealand.

——— (1989). *Consultative Document on the Taxation of Income from Capital*. Wellington, New Zealand.

——— (1998). *The Report to the Treasurer and Minister of Revenue by a Committee of Experts on Tax Compliance*. Wellington, New Zealand.

Capital gains taxation in Mexico and the integration of corporate and personal taxes

FRANCISCO GIL-DÍAZ

Within the economics profession and in journalistic pieces, the taxation of capital gains has been the subject of continuous debate. On one extreme is the Henry-Simons[1] camp that insists on taxing income defined comprehensively, however impracticable, choice distorting, lifecycle inequitable and unrealistic it may be. On the other side is the consumption-based tax camp that includes most modern economists. In the middle is the camp that serves up all kinds of salads depending on the tastes of the proponents (or, to put it more elegantly, social engineers).

This paper will deal first with the tax-base issue to show how far removed from a practical reality is the ideal of so-called comprehensive income taxation. From this conclusion, the jump to consumption-based taxation is natural. But even then, because of the need to recognize the inevitability of the corporate income tax, there is a need to find a solution to the treatment of capital gains on corporate shares if individual consumption (or even income) taxation is to coexist with the corporate income tax. The conclusion is paradoxical and to some it may be somewhat surprising: the only

---

Notes will be found on page 104.

way to avoid the double taxation of gains on corporate shares is to tax them, but to do so in a particular way. The method for treating the taxation of capital gains properly in this context is an old Canadian contribution. It is tax neutral and, therefore, avoids the type of tax arbitrage that concerned The Fraser Institute when it convened the 2000 Symposium on Capital Gains Taxation. But, before discussing this idea, it will be convenient to go into more detail concerning the real-life problems involved with the Simons definition.

Henry Simons´ global income approach

Echoing philosophers' equity ideals, economists have generally favoured progressive taxation as well as an income-tax base with a broad global definition. The required reference to a comprehensive tax base is Henry Simons' *Personal Income Taxation,* where he defines the ingredients required to measure the individual's increase in net worth. Such a concept includes wages, interest, rents, dividends, fringe benefits, subsidies, debt reductions, imputed rent to owner-occupied housing, inheritances, unrealized capital gains, scholarships, gifts, and perhaps even the imputed income of household work. Even while striving towards the attainment of this ideal, policy-makers who claim to have established a global-progressive system of taxation do not realize, or do not confess, how far they are from it, nor how inequitable and random the true incidence of actual income taxation really is.

Theoretical considerations are involved in optimal tax design but the most elaborate and dazzling theoretical construct has to recognize the reality upon which it will be applied. In an interconnected and global environment, policy-makers and politicians should become aware of nasty secrets widely known to taxpayers.

- A substantial portion of top salaries in high-tax countries is deposited in tax havens—just ask high salaried executives in European-based companies about compensation deposits in bank accounts abroad.

- Ingenious and forward-looking tax planning also avoids the fragmentation of large estates and all kinds of complicated ruses disguise substantial capital gains.

- Political lobbying converts income taxes into veritable gruyère cheeses through myriad deductions, concessions, and favourable treatments.

- Fringe benefits often cannot be individualized and taxed or are, because of political considerations, never fully included in the taxable income of individuals.

- In many countries, corporations and non-incorporated firms are taxed differently, with the income of the first frequently subject to double taxation.

- Dividend income is often double taxed or subject to diverse discriminations because of the "evils of distributed earnings."

- Across countries, the individual global income tax, the alleged great equalizer, often accounts for no more than 20% of total fiscal revenues.

- Global corporations readily relocate profits internationally according to tax minimizing strategies.

- A substantial portion of personal income, which stems from the implicit stream of services from owner-occupied housing, is usually not taxed.

- Because of the high mobility of financial capital, interest income is generally not taxed or, when taxed, its burden is shifted to the consumer.

Because of the practical and political reasons given above, the attainment of equity, based on the income tax, is a delusion, a Holy Grail that only serves to inspire the matins of the apostles of global income taxation. So much for the practicality of a comprehensive income tax and the attainability of horizontal and vertical equity.

But how about efficiency considerations? There is a broad consensus in the economics profession that taxes generally distort the choice between labour and leisure but that the income tax also distorts the choice between consumption and savings. A tax that generates equal revenue and comparable equity effects, based on consumption, would be preferable on this account.

The other attribute generally examined in taxes is their incidence and their effect on comparable net of tax incomes. From this perspective, another defect of the income-tax approach is that it views equity from a static point of view. It considers the ideal base for taxation to be all sources of income and the increase in the net wealth of the individual over a given period of time. It is fitting that this approach was perfected in the 1940s, together with the linear-static Keynesian consumption function, which considered current income as the explanatory variable of consumption and totally ignored life-cycle income. With some exceptions, economists tend to ignore the tax design and equity implications of a life-cycle or permanent-income approach to consumption behaviour.

If income is the vehicle towards achieving consumption and if consumption is the quintessential ingredient of a utility function, it is not clear from a theoretical standpoint why income should be the object of taxation instead of consumption. The indirect attainment of an objective, through the taxation of the means instead of the objective itself, might be justified when the objective is hard to define, to administer, or both. But in the case at hand it seems that the opposite is true. Consumption is much easier to tax, unless one wishes to tax consumption directly at the individual level. I return to this issue below.

Intertemporal or life-cycle considerations imply that if consumption is programmed throughout a lifetime in an effort to maximize an individual's utility, it makes sense to target it, instead of global income, as the object of taxation. Beyond practical considerations, income taxation will result in, at best, the equivalent to consumption taxation and, generally, in an inferior outcome. Savings and returns on savings are the tools used by individuals to average out consumption through time. Thus, the life-cycle approach suggests that, if the measure of an individual's utility wealth is consumption, it is the latter that ought to be taxed.

There are practical considerations as well. It is well known that consumption follows a more regular pattern through time than income. Individuals whose income is bunched up, frequently in the early stages of life, as is the case of entertainers, traders, athletes, and so on, face a more progressive income taxation and heavier average taxes than those whose income is more equally distributed through their life-times. The excess tax burden faced by such individuals cannot be eliminated except through extremely complicated lifetime-averaging techniques. The same will usually be true of highly variable incomes derived from such activities as farming, fishing, cattle raising and mining.

The inequities just discussed can be avoided in principle if the tax base and the tax rates are set up so that the present value of tax revenues is the same. Under these conditions, the lifetime incidence of both income and consumption base taxation will be the same and there is no a-priori reason to choose, on equity considerations alone, one tax over the other.

Collection costs are not the determinant of the appropriate choice between consumption and income tax bases. As Hall and Rabushka (1985) point out, consumption taxes can be designed to tax directly an individual or income-based taxes can be designed to be "indirect." On the other hand, collection costs should rather be a decisive factor in the choice between indirect and direct taxation since the collection and compliance costs associated with direct taxes can be considerable. Hall and Rabushka (1985) report a figure of 10% of revenue for the American income tax. However, a tax on wages is one simple direct tax that over the life-cycle is equivalent to taxing consumption.

Given the considerations above, an "income" tax that excludes imputed rents from owner-occupied housing, capital gains and interest income, does not appear to be inequitable but it will be unnecessarily distortive unless it also excludes rental income. Within such a framework, the next section will explore how not to tax capital gains when a corporate tax is in existence.

In summary, efficiency and equity considerations counsel consumption-based taxation because a consumption tax involves a lower number of distorted individual choices and because intertemporal equity is better served. If, on efficiency and intertemporal equity grounds, consumption is to be the preferred mode of taxation, it is evident that capital gains and other sources of capital income ought not to be taxed. One solution to the debate would then be to base taxes on consumption and be done with capital gains taxes.

But, despite all the ink spilt in discussing the theory and the persuasive arguments in favour of consumption taxation, it is a fact of life that a form of income taxation will prevail for a long time to come. Furthermore, and also on practical grounds, imperfect, inefficient, and inequitable taxation of personal income will also prevail to be an extended form of taxation. Under these rules of the game, an important issue to resolve before dealing with the appropriate way to tax corporate capital gains is: should corporate income be taxed twice by having both dividends and capital gains income subject to the income tax

If the answer is negative, the method of avoiding the double taxation of profits is to integrate individual income taxation with corporate income taxation. The exemption of capital gains from the income tax would not be sufficient to avoid double taxation because, under an integrated setup, individuals are entitled to a tax refund if their tax bracket is below that of the corporation. Integration encompasses more than the treatment of dividends. It requires a treatment of gains obtained through the realization of corporate shares symmetrical to the one given to dividends.

The interaction between dividend and capital gains income and its implication for the taxation of capital gains will be the subject of this paper. It will be seen that, to understand the treatment that ought to be given to capital gains income, the two income sources have to be considered jointly. The discussion will deal solely with equity shares and will not include other wealth accretions, such as real estate, art works, or in general the appreciation of any other asset. A succinct presentation of Mexico's perhaps singular experience in this regard will conclude the paper.

Integration of corporate and personal income taxation = disappearance of capital gains

It will be argued that, when dividends are taxed, it is inequitable and inefficient to exempt capital gains. However, it is well known that, if the personal and the corporate income tax are integrated, the tax on dividends will vanish. Under these circumstances, a symmetrical treatment of capital gains requires adjustments to provoke the virtual disappearance of capital gains taxation, as it should under an appropriately balanced non-distorting design. It will be shown that a simple exemption of capital gains will not do and that, paradoxically, a scheme to tax capital gains will, in fact, encourage people to avoid their taxation.

The concern about the taxation of capital gains has at least two origins: the technical, public-finance outlook from which many analysts point out that capital gains are generally overtaxed;[2] and the notion that capital gains are the ultimate manifestation of market, technological, or organizational efforts. As such, these rewards to entrepreneurship ought not even be taxed, lest the motor of economic growth is impaired and welfare reduced.

Digression on inflationary accounting

Before discussing the merits of the diverse modes that capital gains taxation can take, it will be convenient to deal with, and leave aside, the other significant source of double taxation and sometimes even confiscation of capital gains. Over taxation frequently occurs when the purchase price of an asset is not corrected for inflation to calculate its taxable gain. It may even turn into confiscation given a sufficiently high increase in the general price level. A creeping low inflation over a long period is all that is required for this effect to take place.

But, although the remedy for this misfortune seems obvious, beware of individual indexations to correct partial distortions. The reason for these distortions is that general price-level increases will tug at a corporation's balance sheet from different directions and the net result will differ from firm to firm, depending on the relative importance of monetary assets and liabilities. Depending on how several factors combine, corporate profits may be understated or overstated as the result of inflation. If a firm is a net debtor, it gains from inflation on this account, or loses from a net creditor position. The firm also loses from depreciation charges that, being based on the original (nominal) purchase price of capital assets, fall in real terms with inflation. Thus, profits and dividends are, because of inflation, distorted reflections of a firm's true results. This argument is also applicable to any accrued capital gain. While the latter may seem to have ended up being overtaxed in real terms, the gain may be due to inflation that lowered the corporate income tax and resulted in more untaxed reinvested profits. The converse argument also applies, of course: nominal taxation may account for the double taxation of losses!

Could it be that the general impression of over-taxation originates in the isolated perception of taxes? These taxes fall disproportionately on the sale of shares when it would be more appropriate to consider all the inflationary effects on the balance sheet of the firm whose shares were sold.

To conclude this section, it seems wiser to either not index at all or to index comprehensively, that is, to index the whole balance sheet and to carry its adjustments into the taxable profit and losses statement. Partial indexation will introduce an additional source of random variation in end results.

The dilemma—to tax or not to tax capital gains

Excessive capital gains taxation should not be viewed singling out capital gains as a special entity. This is the position of many proponents of capital gains tax reform, especially some vocal contemporary American advocates for the exemption of capital gains from the income tax. Abstracting from the unpredictable effects of inflation, over taxation of capital gains is a result of separate corporate and individual income taxes; it originates in the overall design of the income tax itself. Except for some European countries and Mexico,[3] among others, where the two taxes are integrated, corporate profits are taxed at the firm level and again when they are distributed. In this context, it must be understood that realized capital gains on shares are a form of profit distribution: if an investor decides to sell a corporate share, the proceeds of the sale are equivalent to a "home-made dividend" (Fama and Miller 1972). Therefore, if profits are taxed once at the firm level and again when distributed, symmetry requires that the same base and tax rate be applicable to capital gains.

If distributed profits and capital gains are taxed differently, people will tend to engage in tax arbitrage and to choose the lower taxed vehicle. Therefore, the correct, neutral and equitable goal is not a favoured treatment for capital gains but rather a symmetrical treatment of distributed profits and of capital gains. If the first are taxed twice, so should the other and, if the first are not adjusted for inflation, it is not clear why the other should.

On the other hand, there are no efficiency or equity grounds to double-tax corporate profits, if dividend and corporate profit taxation were integrated; that is, if only the individual shareholder were considered the unit of taxation, capital gains taxation would virtually disappear.

Under such a scheme, a corporate income tax is solely an individual income tax withheld at the source, just as is frequently done with wage or interest income. In this vein, individuals add up their various sources of income, including dividends, albeit grossed-up to determine the profit before corporate income tax, but then the corporate income tax would be creditable as a withheld tax in order to arrive at the individual income tax.

The end result of this procedure is that corporate profits would be taxed only once at the individual's level. Such a design requires parallel corrections in the way capital gains are taxed. The seller of a share would be allowed to modify its purchase price when calculating the difference between the sale and purchase prices to arrive at the taxable capital gain. The required adjustment would be to allow for taxed reinvested profits to be added to the purchase price of the share and to deduct corporate losses. When the individual and the corporation's marginal tax rates differ, a grossing-up and tax-credit procedure similar to the dividend method is required. This method is discussed below.

To simplify the first example, the two rates will be assumed to be equal. In this case, since most capital gains originate in the appreciation of share values derived from the reinvestment of profits, the deduction of these investments from the capital gain should cancel out the capital gains' tax base.

There is a caveat to the last assertion because, beyond the mere reinvestment of profits, a share's value may appreciate because of the market's appraisal of the growth potential of a particular firm, an appreciation beyond the average expected marginal return on other investments. Examples abound, such as Wal-Mart, Microsoft and, until recently, the "dotcoms."

Even in this case, the adjusted purchase-cost procedure outlined above should generate neutrality; that is, no taxation of capital gains or, equivalently, no double taxation of profits. Consider for simplicity (a) no corporate income tax; (b) a firm whose profits are reinvested; (c) a 10% annual discount factor; (c) a riskless environment; and (d) a change of market sentiment so that a share that had been expected to yield the same 10% as the rest of the market is suddenly expected to appreciate 20% the following year. Assume also a $100 purchase price for the share and that, after the 20% appreciation, the share is expected to continue yielding 10% per year. The original purchaser of that share, who paid $100 for it, can now sell it for $109.1 and pay a tax of 91 cents, if we assume a proportional income tax of 10%. If the original holder sells the share immediately after its higher expected return is known to the market and if the new owner sells it at the end of a year for $120, the tax adjusted cost of the share for the latter will be $129.1, since the firm generated and reinvested $20 in profits. The second seller of the share will be able to deduct from his global tax bill losses equal to $9.1, for a tax saving of 91 cents. The capital gains tax paid by the first individual is thus offset, except for the difference in present value, by the tax saving of the second individual, who obtained a 10% return on the purchase plus the tax-saving on a capital-gains deduction.

However, the numbers above cannot be the outcome under a perfect capital market, while the original asset holder obtained an extraordinary return. The unexpected and sudden appreciation of the share also brings the buyer a return higher than 10% if this tax savings is added to the return on the asset. In a competitive capital market, the original holder will ask somewhat more than $109.1 for the shares in order to let the second holder earn a return just equal to 10%. The sale price in this case will be $110. At this price, the second holder will get a $10 return when selling the share after one year, plus a tax saving equal to a 10% tax rate on the difference between the fiscal cost $110 + $20 = $130 and the $120 sale price, or a savings of $1. A return of $11 on a $110 investment is just equal to the market discount rate of 10%. (The method for arriving at this number with this simple set of assumptions is presented in the Appendix.)

What is of interest here is that, even though the original shareholder pays a tax on the capital gain, the net after-tax income will be the same as if there had been no tax. Since the discount rate is 10% and the net increase in the wealth of this individual is $9.1, the return is the same that would obtain if a capital gains tax did not exist. The original shareholder recovers the tax saving of the second asset holder because the sale price of the share is bid up exactly in the amount necessary to recover the tax. In a competitive market, the original shareholder will be able to capture the tax saving that will eventually be realized by the second holder.

Since for simplicity the numerical example assumed away the corporate income tax, it did not illustrate the important point of how to adjust at the individual level for the tax paid by the firm. Another numerical example will take care of this omission. Assume a share valued at $100, a profit of $10, a corporate income tax of $5, and a dividend of $5 to an individual in a 30% tax bracket. The individual will add to other income the grossed-up dividend ($10), calculate the tax ($3), and credit the corporate income tax formerly paid on that dividend ($5) to arrive to a claim of $2 on the Treasury for a total net income from the dividend of $5 + $2 = $7, that amounts to the disappearance of the corporate income tax.

If the corporation does not pay out a dividend and the individual wishes to obtain the same cash income, the procedure is analogous to the mechanism described above. The share will be sold for $105 and its adjusted cost will also be $105. But, this would be the end of the story only if the shareholder pays a marginal tax rate equal to that paid by the corporation. If the rates are different, the individual will be allowed to credit the $5 tax paid by the corporation to a total taxable income augmented by the grossed-up, unadjusted capital gain ($10), in order to generate the same $2 tax refund.

Therefore, even in a case of extraordinary gains, the taxation method proposed ensures that there is no capital-gains tax. This argument is not new: it has simply been forgotten, since it was presented, in a different fashion, in the report by the Royal Canadian Commission on Taxation (known also as the Carter Commission) in the 1950s.

I hope the discussion above helps to clarify some issues on the important and delicate matter of capital gains taxation reform. A change that simply eliminates the taxation of capital gains will contribute to the disappearance of the tax on dividends and of double taxation as well, at least on the shares of those firms with stock-listed shares. But if this is the desired output, why do it through the back door? And, why not adjust the burden of the tax to the lower rate that should be borne by individuals in the lower brackets?

The arguments presented here suggest that the proper solution is to eliminate both income-tax sources simultaneously. Alternatively, if one wishes to benefit lower-income tax payers, one should apply the integration recipe outlined above regarding capital gains and dividend taxation to transform the corporate income tax into a tax on the individual's income. This solution is much preferable to simply abolishing the capital gains tax because its elimination would turn individuals into tax planners engaged in the elimination of the tax on dividends through tax arbitrage. However, the owners of medium-sized and small-sized firms, for which there is not a ready and liquid stock market, would have trouble selling their shares and would, thereby, be stuck with the tax on dividends. Therefore, whoever claims that reduced or zero capital gains taxation is a benefit for the small entrepreneur should concentrate such intellectual efforts elsewhere.

Zero capital gains taxation would also allow the total avoidance of taxation on those firms where, because of differences between their accounting and fiscal accounting rules, capital gains are realized despite no apparent gain. To close this loophole completely it also has to be established, as was done in Mexico, that realized profits, through dividends or capital gains, will be taxed even if they are generally exempt, when they are derived from profits that did not previously pay the corporate profits tax.

However transparent and non-distorting, the integration solution has serious drawbacks. The accounting requirements are complex and many years of information and documentation are needed. Besides, in countries where the estate tax has contributed to place large amounts of corporate shares in the hands of non-profit institutions, the revenue loss from an integration scheme could be large. This latter problem might be dealt with by not having the corporate tax be definitive in the case of shares held by non-profits, and a partial solution to the accounting and computing complexities might be sought in a rate structure low enough for both taxes with equal proportional rates.

The evolution of the capital gains tax in Mexico

The treatment above was not incorporated into Mexican tax legislation in one fell swoop nor were all its ingredients fully implemented. Given the sharp general price increases of the 1970s and an expectation that inflation would continue, it was deemed convenient at the time to correct in real terms the purchase cost of assets. The solution was to include in the legislation a table constructed with the price levels of the former 50 years.

Another reform had to do with the need to correct for the bunching in time of capital gains, since they are not recurrent for most individuals and may, therefore, be taxed at an extremely high marginal rate simply by adding overall gains to the rest of taxable income. Therefore, a simple averaging procedure was introduced to ease the impact of accumulation.

The other important reform was to add reinvested profits—corrected for inflation—to the adjusted purchase cost of a share, after having deducted any losses and distributed profits. The adjustment does not include the credit for taxes paid in excess by the corporation but, as long as the personal and corporate maximum tax rates coincided, the effect of this omission was probably negligible. The top individual rate is reached at relatively low income thresholds so that most shareholders' marginal tax rate was the same as that of the issuing corporations. This is no longer true since 1994, when the corporate rate was brought below the top personal tax rate. Since then, the corporate rate has slid to 30% and the personal rate rose to 40% in January 1999.

The procedures described above apply to assets held by both individuals and firms, except that capital gains in stock-listed shares owned by individuals continue to be exempt in order to avoid administrative complications. The exemption of individually held stock-listed shares from the capital gains tax has been in force for several years with probably no major fiscal consequences, specially given that, up to 1999, the personal dividend tax was fully integrated into the corporate income tax. This is because, if corrections are made for inflation and reinvested profits, the resulting consolidated tax base for the shares of listed corporations turns out to be either minimum or negative, although there are times when sharp increases in the stock-market index suggest otherwise.

When corporate tax rates are below the top individual marginal income tax rates, this exemption allows the tax consequences of the spread between the personal income tax rate and the corporate tax to be either avoided or deferred. This is done through limiting dividend distribution and letting shareholders obtain their income through exempt capital gains. However, as the top personal marginal income tax rate came to equal the corporate income rate, the incentive to switch the gain into the shares of unlisted companies disappeared. But, the distortion has reappeared under the recent Zedillo reforms that lowered the corporate tax to 34%, reintroduced double taxation through a dividend tax, and raised the top individual marginal tax to 40%.

Before the recent Zedillo reforms, the changes performed on the capital gains tax were intended to improve fairness and to "lubricate" the capital market. An efficient capital market is of utmost importance for sound resource allocation. The former tax on nominal gains led to the strangling of asset transactions because individuals and firms preferred to hold on to their assets rather than incur a tax on gains that were merely nominal. By showing their portfolio valuations at current market prices and excluding potential liabilities stemming from the tax due on the sale of the assets, firms could also better leverage their balance sheets.

As explained above, the capital gains mode of taxation is simply a reflection of an integration procedure adopted between the individual and corporate income taxes, a reform that was aimed at improving both fairness and efficiency.

Initially, the procedure allowed firms to deduct paid dividends just like any other deductible item or cost. It also required a withholding tax at the maximum marginal rates on individual income, creditable by the recipients. The same procedure was applied to interest paid to individuals.

Transfers of dividends among firms were also deductible and cumulative, which allowed interrelated firms to offset losses instantaneously from one side of their operation against gains on the other. This possibility was deemed particularly important within an inflationary environment.

Another reason to adopt an integration formula using a dividend deduction is that, in the first stage of the reform effort, an integration scheme based on an imputation method was introduced. This proved complicated for taxpayers and was later abandoned. Subsequently, when corporate and top personal income tax rates were aligned, the dividend deduction was replaced by a dividend exemption.

With the enactment of these reforms and price stability, the distortion that encouraged debt financing over equity financing was virtually corrected. With inflation, however, the deductibility of real-debt amortization through interest payments created an enormous attraction to issue corporate debt until the tax treatment of both interest income and expense was corrected for inflation.

Appendix

Assumptions and Definitions

- Let V_0 be the purchase price paid by the original owner of the share.
- Let V_0^1 be the sale price after a new higher return is announced. The new return higher (g per year) than previously expected is known by the market seconds after V_0 was paid for the share.
- Let r be the discount rate and "normal" rate of return in the market.
- t is the average and marginal tax rate equal for everybody.
- The sale price V_1 of the share after one year will be

$$V_1 = V_0(1+g)$$

$$\frac{V_1 - t[V_1 - (V_0^1 + gV_0)]}{V_0^1} = 1 + r$$

$$\frac{V_1 - tV_1 + tV_0^1 + tgV_0}{V_0^1} = 1 + r$$

$$V_1 - tV_1 + tV_0^1 + tgV_0 = (1+r)V_0^1$$

$$V_1(1-t) + tgV_0 = (1+r)V_0 - tV_0^1$$

$$V_1(1-t) + tgV_0 = (1+r-t)V_0^1$$

$$V_0^1 = \frac{V_1(1-t) + tgV_0}{1+r-t} = \frac{V_0(1+g)(1-t) + tgV_0}{1+r-t}$$

$$V_0^1 = \frac{V_0(1+g)(1-t) + tg}{1+r-t}$$

Notes

1 The classic reference for a comprehensive income taxation definition is Simons 1938.
2 The postponement of the gain does not lower the present value of the tax. See Gil Díaz 1982.
3 This comment is no longer fully applicable to Mexico where recent reforms have destroyed the former symmetry and neutrality of its combined personal and corporate income-tax structure.

References

Carter Commision (1966). *Report of the Royal Commission on Taxation (Volume 3): Taxation of Income*. Ottawa: Queen's Printer.

Fama, Eugene, and Merton Miller (1972). *The Theory of a Finance*. New York: Holt, Richard & Winston.

Gil Díaz, Francisco (1982). *Three Essays on the Taxation of Capital*. Ph.D. dissertation, Faculty of the Division of the Social Sciences, University of Chicago (December, 1982).

―― (1993). *Política Fiscal y Administración Tributaria: La Experiencia de México*. Subsecretaría de Ingresos.

―― (1996). To Tax or Not Tax: That Is *Not* the Question, But How to Tax Best. Unpublished paper given at Conference at the International Tax Program, Harvard University (June 3, 1996).

Gil Díaz, Francisco, and Wayne Thrisk (2000). Mexico's Protracted Tax Reform. *Gaceta de Economía-ITAM* (January).

Hall, Robert, and Alvin Rabushka (1985). *The Flat Tax*. Stanford, CA: Hoover Institution Press.

Simons, Henry (1938). *Personal Income Taxation*. Chicago: University of Chicago Press.

3 Capital gains tax regimes abroad—countries with inflation indexing

Capital gains taxation in Britain
The merits of indexing and tapering

BARRY BRACEWELL-MILNES

The capital gains tax was introduced in the United Kingdom under the Finance Act, 1965. It was consolidated in the Capital Gains Tax Act of 1979 and the Taxation of Chargeable Gains Act of 1992. These dates imply that non-trading capital gains were not subject to tax for more than a 150 years after income tax was brought in by Addington at the beginning of the nineteenth century. This late introduction of the capital gains tax is in stark contrast with the experience of the United States, where the Federal income tax was levied on capital gains from the beginning.

In the early years of the Second World War, Britain's maximum rate of income tax was increased to the sacrificial level of 19s 6d in the pound (97.5% gross) as a contribution to the war effort. After the war, this increase was treated as politically irreversible. It was not until 35 years after the war ended that the reforming government of Margaret Thatcher lowered this rate.

In the early 1960s, the gap between tax at 97.5% on income and 0% on capital gains was uncomfortably wide and increasingly exploited. Instead of reducing income tax, the Labour government, that was elected in 1964 introduced a tax on capital gains. This new

---

Notes will be found on page 121.

tax on individuals was set at 30%. The difference in the two rates of taxation represents a tacit admission of the economic difference between income and capital gains.

The capital gains tax rate on individuals remained at 30% for more than 20 years. In 1988, Chancellor of the Exchequer Lawson introduced a new rate structure. Capital gains were to be added to income and charged at the marginal rate of income tax. In practice, this was usually the top rate of income tax, which by 1988 had been reduced to 40%. Thus, capital gains and the top tranche of income were taxed respectively in 1964 at zero and 97.5%; in 1965 at 30% and 97.5% and in 1988 at 40% and 40%.

A company's chargeable gains have been treated since 1965 as part of its profits for corporation tax and charged at the appropriate rate. In 1965, this rate was limited to 30%, as for individuals. Trustees are subject to the same regime as individuals. Gifts are taxable unless they are made to a spouse or a charity; holdover relief for gifts between individuals was abolished in 1989. Emigration is a taxable event for companies but not for individuals. The charge on death was abolished for deaths occurring after 31 March 1971.

Gilt-edged stocks were exempted from capital gains taxes in 1969 if they were held for more than one year; this twelve-month qualifying period was removed in 1986. Certain corporate bonds were likewise made exempt assets in 1986. Financial institutions like unit trusts are not subject to capital gains tax, although their unit holders are. As a result, there is a strong incentive to own shares indirectly through a financial institution. Quoted companies do not on the whole pay much corporation tax on capital gains as they have more scope than individuals for tax reduction through appropriate planning. Owner-managers of unquoted companies and other businesses incur a tax liability on transfers of the business *inter vivo*. Holdover relief, which was retained for business assets in 1989, is not an exemption, and the tax charge held over may constitute an important liability for the business as well as for the owners.

The preceding summary of capital gains taxation in Britain implies that it is primarily a charge on individuals and trustees, partly because of the explicit concessions and tax privileges for companies. One of these concessions, rollover relief for the replacement of business assets, was introduced in 1971, whereas there is no general rollover relief for individuals. The rationale for this policy is based on differences between a natural and a corporate person: an individual has a life-cycle, which may generate taxable events, whereas a corporation is in principle undying. In addition, if an individual owns a company that makes a capital gain, the gain is taxed twice, first through the company and second on the owner upon the sale of the appreciated shares.

Indexation

In the late 1970s, price inflation rose to its highest level at well over 25% a year. Capital gains taxation under the 1965 provisions did not adjust rates for inflation. It was feared that the tax would cause serious damage to the economy since the taxation of inflationary capital gains amounts to the confiscation of real assets. In response to this threat, in October 1977 the Inland Revenue issued for comment and discussion a note that examined the administrative aspects of tapering, indexation, and other schemes to take account of the distortionary effects of capital gains taxes on highly inflated asset values.

After the 1979 Election, the new Conservative government addressed the problems caused by inflation, slowly and cautiously at first. In 1982, an indexation allowance was introduced for inflation after that year. The indexation was based on historic cost, which might have been incurred many years earlier, and a small proportion of the current value. The indexation could not be applied for gains during the first year of ownership and was not available if it created a loss or increased a loss that already existed (see Soper 1997: 18).

In 1985, the tax relief based on the use of indexation was extended backwards to the date of acquisition and the taxpayer was given the choice of using either historic cost or the value on March 31, 1982. In addition, the allowance could now be given on assets sold at a loss and could be used to create a loss. In 1988, the rate of capital gains tax was made equal to the rates of tax on individual incomes and corporate profits. At the same time, the government offered the further beneficial option of rebasing the cost of assets to March 31, 1982. Thus, while in 1985 taxpayers were permitted to use the value on March 31, 1982 to calculate the indexation allowance, in 1988 they were permitted to use this date as the date of acquisition. This meant that pre-1982 gains were disregarded in the calculation of capital gains for the purpose of taxation. However, if it was to their advantage, taxpayers were still permitted to use the original date of acquisition rather than March 31, 1982 as the base for indexation (see Soper 1997: 18).

In 1998, the new Labour government froze indexation for disposals by individuals after April 5, 1998. However, the new law permitted the submission of returns filed after this date if they contained indexation for earlier years. The indexation regime for corporate taxpayers remained unaltered (*Financial Times Information Capital Gains Tax Service* 1982/83–1999/2000: xviii). The 1998 law replaced indexation for individuals and trustees by a system of "tapering," under which the rate of capital gains taxation was made a decreasing function of the length of time over which an asset was held. Individuals' retirement relief from capital gains tax was phased out at the same time. The tapering system introduced in 1998 was made more generous for taxpayers in legislation passed in 2000 in ways that will be discussed below in the section, Indexation and tapering.

Indexation is based on the Retail Prices Index, which is a Laspeyres base-weighted index computed from a basket of goods and services covering about half of national income. A Retail Prices Index Advisory Committee advises the government about changes in the basket and other modifications. The Retail Prices Index is familiar to the public and is published about six weeks after the end of the period it covers. For these reasons, it has proved resistant to radical reform and is used in various parts of the tax system. The existing Retail Prices Index is widely criticized because increases in interest rates and indirect taxes, often caused by attempts to cool the economy and check inflation, feed into the Retail Prices Index and thus initially show inflation as rising. For this reason, the government publishes an "underlying" Retail Prices Index from which these elements are excluded. But, this procedure causes the underlying rate to exceed the most widely used "headline" index if interest rates fall. More recent criticisms of the Retail Prices Index are that in periods of rapid technological innovation the index exaggerates inflation by not allowing for improvements in the quality of goods and services consumed. It is also suspected that sometimes governments manipulate the Retail Prices Index to their own political advantage.[1]

In spite of these shortcomings of the Retail Prices Index in the use of calculating capital gains tax allowances, there is little support in the United Kingdom for the construction or use of a new index. Such a switch would bring only minor benefits at best. Over the period from 1982 to 1998, indexation served the useful purpose of reducing the lock-in effect and generally reducing the burden of a damaging tax.

The most important criticism of indexation of any kind arises from the fact that it is basically anti-entrepreneurial. Goodwill, the most entrepreneurial element of the sale of a new business, does not benefit from indexation since its acquisition cost is nil. The use of indexation can also be criticized on the grounds that there are other, superior means for reducing the burden of capital gains taxation. These alternatives will be discussed below.

Pooling

If taxpayers buy a given company's shares only once, the value of capital gains can be established readily upon the sale of some or all holdings. Presumably, the 1965 Inland Revenue thought that most taxpayers buy shares in a company only once and add to their portfolio through the purchase of shares of other companies. But, it has since been discovered that investors are as likely to increase holdings of a given company's shares as they are to diversify. Additions to the holdings of a given company's share at different times gives rise to the problem of identifying the cost of the shares sold and bringing a capital gain.

Three methods of identification are in common use: first in, first out (FIFO); last in, first out (LIFO); and pooling (which is the technical term for averaging in this context). If shares rise in value, through unindexed inflation or in real terms, LIFO is more favourable to the taxpayer than pooling and pooling is more favourable than FIFO. If share prices fall, these relationships are reversed. If the share prices are constant, all three methods are equivalent.

However, under Britain's system of tapering, the ranking is more complicated. Constant prices produce the same ordering for the merit of the available accounting methods as do falling prices. Rising prices make the ranking ambiguous.

Britain now has the rule that all shares of a given company acquired by a taxpayer are pooled if they were acquired after April 6, 1965 and before the introduction of indexation on April 6, 1982.[2] Any form of identification chosen by the taxpayer or the company for individual shares (as, for example, the numbers in a register) is irrelevant under the pooling system. Securities of different classes (as, for example, ordinary shares and convertible preference shares of the same company) are held in separate pools. Shares held in different capacities (as, for example, beneficial ownership and trusteeship) are likewise held in separate pools (Walker 1994: 17).

Shares acquired before April 1965 continue to be held thereafter in the separate parcels by which they were acquired. However, in 1968 Inland Revenue allowed taxpayers the option of electing for post-1968 disposals to have pre-1965 holdings pooled with post-1965 acquisitions of shares of the same class and held in the same capacity. Under this option, the taxpayers are deemed to have sold the shares on April 6, 1965 and to have immediately re-acquired them on the same day at the day's market value. From April 6, 1965 until April 5, 1968 and thereafter, if the election to pool was not made, pre-1965 shares were taken up to meet subsequent disposals on a first-in-first-out basis (FIFO) until 1982 when that basis was reversed to last-in-first-out (LIFO) (Walker 1994: 15, 21).

As noted above, a limited form of indexation was introduced in April 1982 and lasted until April 1985. During this three-year period, pooling was discontinued. Instead, each acquisition of shares was treated separately for purposes of indexation. New identification rules applied during this three-year period to disposals of part, but not all, of post-1982 acquisitions. The general direction of the identification rules of 1982 to 1985 was to work backward (LIFO) until the disposal was satisfied. But, the opposite (FIFO) rule was applied if a part disposal did not use up the whole of the acquisitions in the 12 months immediately preceding the sale (Walker 1994: 22, 23).

Share pooling was reintroduced under the Finance Act, 1985 for shares and securities acquired on or after, for individuals, April 6, 1982 and, for companies, April 1, 1982. In order to take the indexation allowance into account, an addition is made to the pool of expenditure associated with the post-April 5, 1982 holding whenever there is any kind of transaction like an acquisition, disposal, or rights issue of the shares concerned. This addition is computed by multiplying the value of the pool immediately before the transaction by the increase in the Retail Prices Index over the period from the date of the last transaction (*Financial Times Information Capital Gains Tax Service* 1982/1983–1999/2000: xv-xvi).

The introduction of taper relief for individuals and trustees but not for companies meant that pooling must cease for acquisitions on or after April 6, 1998. There are new identification provisions. Disposals on or after April 6, 1998 are now generally to be identified on a LIFO basis. This regulation reduces the advantage of taper relief, which increases the longer the asset is held (Chamberlain 1998: 474).

Capital losses

The end of "the use of indexation to create or increase capital gains tax losses" was announced in the Budget Speech on November 30, 1993. The Budget press release (IR28) notes: "Indexation will continue to be available to reduce a gain to nil if appropriate. But it will not be available to increase, or create, an allowable capital loss." The changes applied to all disposals and to the treatment of "no gain/no loss" transfers, such as between spouses or companies, made on Budget Day or thereafter. In response to representations, a measure of transitional relief was announced on April 15. It provides that up to 10,000 pounds of indexation loss could be used to reduce capital gains tax liabilities for 1993/1994 and 1995/1996 combined.[3]

The scope of indexation relief was extended to losses in 1985. In his Budget speech, Chancellor Lawson said: "(Indexation) relief, valuable though it is, and increasingly valuable as it will become, suffers from three serious limitations … Second, the indexation does not at present extend to losses. I propose to remove this restriction." The reimposition of the restriction was all the more serious since the rate of tax levied on most individuals' gains had been increased to 40%.

The government always claimed that the restriction of capital loss indexation was an anti-avoidance measure but the nature of this avoidance was disclosed only gradually and with a lag. Thus, the Financial Secretary to the Treasury, Stephen Dorrell, MP, only three and one-half months after the Budget speech identified three types of alleged abuse. The first was the retention of assets of negligible value. The second was the exchange of assets within groups of companies so as to create an indexed loss to which there was no commercial counterpart. The third was the sale and purchase of capital-certain bonds, subject to capital gains taxation even though the gain is predetermined.

The yield of capital gains tax on individuals and trustees was 1.0 billion pounds in 1993/1994 and 1.3 billion pounds in 1994/1995. The restriction of loss relief was estimated to yield 300 million pounds in 1996/1997 and to rise to 3 billion pounds by the end of the decade. Two thirds of the increased yield was expected to come from companies and one third from individuals. The method for computing these figures was not published and they evoked widespread public scepticism.

Few tax changes were so widely and vigorously condemned by business and tax professionals as were the 1993 changes to the indexation of capital losses. It was argued that the alleged abuses should have been targeted, that the 40% rate of capital gains tax paid by most individuals was internationally high, and that the restriction of loss relief made the effective rate far higher. In addition, the restriction increased risk-aversion and passive investment. The capital gains tax was already biased in the government's favour since the yield was always positive even if taxpayers collectively had made a loss. The restriction of loss relief made this bias even worse. In fact, the alleged abuses were economically justifiable methods for even-handed treatment of gains and losses.

The government argued that it was impossible to have a system of indexation that preserved the neutrality of gains and losses: "I am presenting a critique of the 1985 loss indexation provisions, not on the grounds that they are wrong in principle, but that when they are applied in practice, they create opportunities for exactly the sort of abuse that I have described" (The Financial Secretary to the Treasury in Standing Committee on March 15, 1994 [*Hansard*, col. 701]). However, these practical difficulties were never explained and many argued that if they did exist, neutrality should have been achieved by the provision of some other policies and rules.

The restriction of loss relief raises the effective rate of capital gains taxation above the nominal rate for taxpayers in general. In addition, it does so particularly for taxpayers who can least afford it, because they have suffered losses. It therefore turns the concept of taxable capacity upside down. It violates horizontal equity by different treatment of taxpayers in like situations and it violates vertical equity by taxing the poorer taxpayer more heavily than the richer.

Capital gains and income

The Haig-Simons definition of income, in which capital gains are income as much as personal income or dividends, is, in theory, based on the accrual of capital gains. In practice, it is based on the realization of gains. According to Simons: "A solid structure of income-tax legislation must ultimately reach all gains in the hands of the person to whom they accrue." However, "the proper underlying conception of income cannot be directly and fully applied in the determination of year-to-year assessments. Outright abandonment of the realization criterion would be utter folly." But, Simons accepted the realization criterion reluctantly and grudgingly: "The real culprit here is the realization criterion ... One may complain of this practice; but to demand that it be abandoned outright is to display little regard for practical considerations ... Unfortunately, the realization criterion must be accepted as a practical necessity" (Simons 1938: 168, 207, 153).

Realization rather than accrual is responsible for the propensity of investors to hold on to appreciated assets with lower yields than are available through alternative investments. This effect is due to the reduction in the investible sums caused by the payment of the tax on the capital gains. Thus, capital gains taxation results in the so-called lock-in effect, which leads to inefficiencies in the allocation of capital.

There is another important reason why accrued capital gains are a poor basis for taxation. Without the sale of an asset, it is very difficult to establish the value of such assets as paintings, antiques, and similar unique goods. Only arms-length transactions can reveal the true market prices of such assets. The valuation of financial assets is complicated by the purchase of shares at different times and prices and increases in value due to rights issues, takeovers, amalgamations, and the like.

Under expenditure taxation, both investment income and capital gains are excluded from the tax base and tax is payable only on the amount spent on goods and services. Under income taxation, investment income is included in the taxable base. Capital gains taxation goes one stage further than the income tax. It includes not only the income stream from capital but also the capital value of any increase in the income stream. Capital taxation thus involves the anticipation of the additional income tax that would be payable in due time on the additional income. In this sense, it amounts to the confiscation of a substantial part of what would otherwise be an increase of capital in private hands.

I have argued elsewhere (Bracewell-Milnes 1982: 24) that, as income and wealth increase, consumption increases less rapidly. Wealth in private hands becomes less and less a source of future spending power and more and more a form of ownership of productive assets. Saving for future consumption is gradually replaced by saving in perpetuity. Individuals do not generally lose interest in additional wealth merely because they already have all they require for consumption.

The foregoing differences between income and capital gains lead to a wide difference between the revenue-maximizing rates for income and capital gains taxes. In Bracewell-Milnes (1993), I used the concepts of the Dupuit or Laffer curve to estimate that the revenue-maximizing rate of capital gains tax in the United Kingdom is of the order of 15%. The revenue-maximizing rate of income tax must be considerably higher. As Hesiod says, "Fools, and they know not how much the half exceeds the whole" (*Works and Days* 40).

Income and capital gains are as distinct as day and night, even though there are short periods of ambiguity at dawn and dusk. If it were right to tax capital gains as income, indexation would merely remove the additional burden imposed by price rises. But, I believe that it is not right to tax capital gains as income. In my view, therefore, indexation lightens the burden of an excessive and damaging tax. As such, it reduces public demands for the elimination of the unjust tax and it prevents to adoption of superior alternative methods like tapering for reducing the burden.

Indexation and tapering

Indexation was frozen in the Budget of March 1998 for individuals and trustees, though not for companies, and retirement relief was phased out. Introduced was a system of tapering, which reduced the rate of capital gains charged the longer an asset was held. In practice, this effect is achieved by reductions in the percentage of capital gains subject to tax. The exact rate of tapering in 1995 is given in table 1.

In the Budget of March 2000, the taper was shortened for business assets disposed of after April 5, 2000, although the finishing rate remained the same.[4] Table 2 shows these new tapering rates and the effective taxation rates they give rise to.

From April 6, 2000 onward, employee shareholdings in all trading companies and all shareholdings in unquoted trading companies qualify for the business-asset taper. There is a 5% minimum qualifying holding for quoted trading companies. The previous 5% minimum for unquoted trading companies is abolished.

The relative merits of indexation and tapering have been discussed publicly for more than 20 years, even before the October 1977 publication of the Inland Revenue's note. Some business groups, like the Institute of Directors, had supported tapering against indexation throughout this period. The Conservative government of 1979 to

Table 1: The taper of capital gains taxes in 1998

Holding period (years)	Percentage of gain chargeable on personally held business assets	Percentage of gain chargeable on personally held non-business assets
0	100.0	100
1	92.5	100
2	85.0	100
3	77.5	95
4	70.0	90
5	62.5	85
6	55.0	80
7	47.5	75
8	40.0	70
9	32.5	65
10+	25.0	60

Table 2: Taper on capital gains taxes on business assets in 2000

Holding period (years)	Percentage of gain chargeable on personally held business assets	Effective tax rate (%) Higher rate taxpayer	Effective tax rate (%) Basic-rate taxpayer
0	100	40	20
1	87.5	35	17.5
2	75	30	15
3	50	20	10
4+	25	10	5

1997 had not overcome Inland Revenue hostility to tapering and the outgoing Chancellor in 1997, Kenneth Clarke, was particularly unsympathetic. (For a longer history of this controversy, see Bracewell-Milnes 1978.)

The economically most important effects of tapering are that it increases the lock-in effect during the period of taper but reduces it thereafter. This analysis suggests that to minimize the harmful effect of tapering, the rate of tapering should be rapid and end in a zero rate of tax.

Critics of indexation fall into two categories. First, there are the supporters of comprehensive income taxation who regard indexation as an unnecessary complication. For example, in a passage that encapsulates his confusing position on the subject of taxing capital gains, Henry Simons says: "Considerations of justice demand that changes in monetary conditions be taken into account in the measurement of gain and loss. As soon as one begins to translate this generalization into actual procedures, however, one comes quickly to the conviction that some things are well let alone" (Simons 1938: 155). In a similar vein, Leonard Burman devotes a chapter of a work on capital gains taxation to arguing against indexing capital gains for inflation.

Indexation is also criticized by a second group of analysts who have little or no sympathy for comprehensive income taxation. These analysts argue that the indexation of capital gains tax makes a bad tax seem less burdensome and economically damaging. It thus increases its public acceptability. This group also opposes indexing on the grounds that it is a substitute for other measures to account for inflation, especially tapering, which encourage abolition.[5]

Friends and enemies of a capital gains tax based on comprehensive income taxation are found at all points of the political spectrum. There are few topics on which supporters and opponents of the free market are so much at odds among themselves.

Difficulties of the present system

Difficulties inherent in the present system of capital gains taxation are discussed above under the headings *Indexation, Pooling,* and *Capital losses*. Capital gains taxation has never been a tax at ease with itself and its history since the 1960s has been one of changes leading to demands for further changes.

Capital gains taxation has always caused difficulties for the choice of business organization, be it a sole ownership, partnership, or a corporation, privately held or publicly traded. The corporate type of organization leaves the proprietors subject to unrelieved double taxation, first, at the level of the corporation and, then, at the level of the proprietors. Special problems arise from the fact that corporate gains are indexed while gains accruing to individuals are subject to tapering, and at different rates for business and non-business assets to boot. This different treatment of income from corporations and individuals conflicts with the long-standing principle of British tax law that corporations and individuals should as far as possible be subject to the same or similar regimes.

There was a temporary but serious difficulty when tapering was brought in for individuals but retirement relief was removed. The combination of these measures was to the advantage of taxpayers at the higher end of the capital scale but substantially to the disadvantage of taxpayers in the middle. The problem was mitigated when the period of taper was shortened for business assets in March 2000.

The changes in capital gains taxation over the years have added layer after layer of complexity. The tax is unintelligible to the general public, and it is the only tax on which many tax professionals regularly seek professional advice from a few highly specialized colleagues.

Capital gains taxation does not yield much revenue and does not affect many taxpayers, partly because it is avoided by many through proper tax planning. Past experience suggests that there would be little political reaction to the abolition of the tax or substantial changes to measures that reduce the effective tax burden through indexing, tapering, or other such policies.

Business and the professions, including professionals who make money from the tax, are widely critical of the complexity and administrative costs of the tax. They are sympathetic to a variety of measures aimed at reducing the tax and administrative burden. Unfortunately, however, there is little consensus about specific policy changes.

The direction of reform

The main thesis of this chapter is that capital gains taxation is an economically damaging tax. There is growing international consensus that it should be abandoned. If such a radical solution is not possible, it is better to have measures to reduce its burden and inefficiencies, like indexation or tapering.[6]

However, these two measures do not have equal merit. Those who view capital gains as necessary for reasons of equity and efficiency consider indexation desirable. Indexation makes the tax fairer and less distorting. Tapering generally appeals to those who believe it desirable to have low rates of taxation to minimize the efficiency cost, especially the lock-in effect. Tapering, which ultimately lowers the tax to zero, appeals most to those who oppose the Simons definition of income. These analysts, including myself, believe that capital gains are distinctly different from other sources of income and, in particular, that all certain gains should be taxed and uncertain gains should not.

Notes

1. According to Anne Segall, in an article written for *The Daily Telegraph* (June 8, 2000),

   > [t]he ability of politicians to fudge figures or bury uncomfortable facts should become a thing of the past after the launch yesterday of National Statistics, an umbrella body which will take control of all the statistics produced by government departments as well as those currently produced by the Office for National Statistics.
   >
   > The aim is to end controversy over the reliability of sensitive data on issues such as hospital waiting lists, classroom sizes and crime levels. Despite initial reservations, ministers have agreed to relinquish control over the data collected within their departments to Britain's first ever National Statistician.
   >
   > Len Cook, a 50-year-old New Zealander with ambitions to make British statistics "among the best in the world," has been recruited. He will review the way government departments collect, analyse and publish figures to ensure that they meet the standards demanded by National Statistics. Only then will departments be allowed to publish their findings under the National Statistics brand, which is intended to be a symbol of integrity and reliability.

2. For companies the date is April 1, 1982. It does not matter whether the shares were acquired through purchase or inheritance.
3. This section of the paper is based on the more extensive treatment of capital losses in Bracewell Milnes 1994.
4. From 1999/2000, gains are charged at 20% where the gains when added to total income are below the basic rate limit and at 40% where they exceed that limit.
5. Tapering is one of six "reductions in capital gains tax compatible with its abolition" mentioned in Bracewell-Milnes 1992.
6. For elaboration on these points, see Barry Bracewell-Milnes 1992.

References

Bracewell-Milnes, Barry (1978). United Kingdom Capital Gains Tax: Indexation versus Tapering Relief. *Intertax 4*.
——— (1982). *Land and Heritage: The Public Interest in Personal Ownership*. London: Institute of Economic Affairs.
——— (1992). Capital Gains Tax: Reform through Abolition. In *A Discredited Tax: The Capital Gains Tax Problem and Its Solution* (London: Institute of Economic Affairs).
——— (1992). Capital Gains Tax: The Case for Competition. *Intertax* (November).
——— (1993). *False Economy: The Losses from High Capital Gains Tax Rates*. London: Adam Smith Institute
——— (1994). Indexation of Capital Losses: The Price of Principle. *British Tax Review* (May).
Chamberlain, Emma, (1998). Finance Act Notes. *British Tax Review.*
Financial Times Information Capital Gains Tax Service 1982/1983–1999/2000.
Segall, Anne (2000). *The Daily Telegraph* (8 June).
Soper, Paul (1997). *How to Avoid Paying Capital Gains Tax*. London: Rushmere Wynne.
Simons, Henry (1938). *Personal Income Taxation*. Chicago: Chicago University Press.
Walker, G.C. Philip (1994). In Barry Rose (ed.), *Capital Gains Tax: Indexation of Shares and Securities.*

Indexation and Australian capital gains taxation

JOHN FREEBAIRN

Broad-based capital gains taxation was introduced in Australia in 1985 as a component of measures to improve efficiency, equity and revenue security by broadening the income base. From September 1985 to November 1999, realized capital gains were subject to normal income tax rates. In 1996/1997, capital gains taxes collected $2.1 billion, equivalent to 2.3% of total income-tax revenue or about 0.4% of GDP. In 1999, indexation of capital gains was removed and the tax rate halved in what was claimed to be a roughly revenue-neutral package that would stimulate Australian capital markets.

This chapter follows the rise and fall of indexation in the measurement of taxable capital gains in Australia. It describes the processes and reasons for the policy changes, gives details of the operation of capital gains taxation, and comments on the efficiency, equity, simplicity, and revenue outcomes under different policy regimes. The chapter follows a chronological path, beginning in the first section with a discussion of capital gains taxation before 1985. The following two sections deal with the 1985 reforms and their effects. The concluding three sections analyze the 1999 reforms and their expected effects and provide an overall assessment.

Notes will be found on page 139.

Capital gains taxation before 1985

Prior to 1985, the taxation of capital gains in Australia was very limited, with effectively only two areas of taxation. Under the Income Tax and Assessment Act, Sc 26AAA provided for the taxation of most profits on the sale of property within one year of purchase and Sc 25A provided for taxation of profits made from the sale of property acquired for the purpose of profit-making by sale. This is essentially the taxation regime currently operating in Hong Kong and New Zealand and described in other chapters. In practice, with the exemption of trading stock and for registered dealers and traders, Sc 25A was not effective as taxpayers could easily avoid the "profit-making incentive." In other words, prior to 1985, most capital gains on property held for more than 12 months were not subject to income taxation or to special capital gains taxation.

Capital gains taxation before 1985 was not without its problems. There were incentives to shift investment returns from "income" to "capital gains" to reduce tax obligations. Numerous legal cases were fought in defining the gray line between investment returns and capital gains. Tax-avoidance schemes based on the surplus-stripping model described by Grubel in Part 1 were developed: the most notorious were dubbed "bottom-of-the-harbour schemes." The use of such tax avoidance raised serious questions about integrity and general confidence in the total taxation system.

The 1985 debate and change

In 1985, the Labour government responded to community concerns about the need for tax reforms through a Draft White Paper (1985), a Summit on Taxation Reform and, ultimately, a number of policy changes (given in Keating 1985). The Draft White Paper focused on better ways of collecting about the same aggregate revenue while making the system fairer, more conducive to a productive economy, and more secure as a source of revenue.

Three packages of changes were proposed in the Draft White Paper as options for consideration at the Summit on Taxation Reform. Option A consisted of a number of measures for broadening the income base, including a broad-based capital gains tax, a fringe benefits tax, a national identification scheme, and the removal of several concessions. The additional proceeds from these changes were to be used to fund lower rates of income taxation.

Option B added a 5% retail sales tax (dubbed a broad-based consumption tax) to achieve some rationalization of existing indirect taxes and a small shift in the tax mix towards consumption. Option C proposed measures for broadening the income-tax base and a larger 12.5% retail sales tax to effect a more substantial tax mix change and lower marginal income tax rates.

The government's preferred Option C was taken to the Summit where it was not well received. However, there was considerable support for a package of measures for broadening the income base and for lower tax rates along the lines proposed in Option A. Later in 1985, the government passed a significantly modified income-tax reform package, which included lower income-tax rates and the introduction of the capital gains tax

In 1985, the case for effective and explicit taxation of capital gains rested primarily on the argument that it broadened the income-tax base and moved the entire system to a closer approximation of a comprehensive income tax base. To quote the Draft White Paper: "The case for taxing income in the form of capital gains thus follows from the general case for comprehensiveness in the definition of the income tax base and is similarly grounded in terms of objectives of equity, efficiency and combating tax avoidance" (1985: 77). The Draft White Paper elaborated on each of these public finance objectives. Thus, the capital gains tax would improve vertical equity since the ownership of capital, and the receipt of capital gains, are heavily concentrated among higher income groups. It would improve vertical and horizontal equity by removing the favourable treatment enjoyed under the old regime by people whose income includes capital gains.

The previously existing hybrid tax systems imposed different effective tax rates on different saving and investments. It was, therefore, considered obvious that the new taxation of capital gains would improve efficiency and no explicit arguments were offered to make this case. The greatest source of efficiency gains stemmed from the lower marginal tax rates funded by the measures for broadening the income base, including capital gains.[1] Other important arguments advanced for capital gains taxation were that it would reduce tax avoidance[2] and secure future revenue by reducing the incentives to convert otherwise taxable income into nontaxable capital gains.

After the decision to tax capital gains had been taken in principle, a number of practical rules about capital gains taxation were debated. The theoretical appeal of taxation of accrued capital gains gave way to a number of practical considerations for a tax only on realized capital gains. Gifts are treated as a realization. The Draft White Paper argued that death should also be deemed as a point of realization. However, the accepted legislation reflected political pressures, especially from the rural and small-business sector, and death was not considered to trigger capital gains and their taxation.

Initially, it was proposed that all assets owned in 1985 should be subject to taxation of capital gains realized upon their sale but the final legislation applied a grandfather clause and made taxable only gains on property acquired after September 19, 1985. Owner-occupied homes, most personal chattels, superannuation paid out to individuals, and the proceeds of life-insurance polices were exempted from the capital gains tax.

Debates over the taxation of nominal rather than real capital gains were resolved by a mixed package of legislation. In the case of assets held for less than 12 months, the nominal gains are taxable. Assets held for more than 12 months are taxed only on real gains and capital additions. Nominal gains are converted into real gains by deflation with the general consumer price index. By contrast, only nominal losses, not real losses, can be used as an offset against real capital gains. Nominal losses can be carried forward. Nominal gains not large enough to be real gains are neither taxable nor deductible.

The final package of taxation of real capital gains and deduction of nominal capital losses represents a political compromise and emerged from the following somewhat contradictory arguments in the Draft White Paper. On the one hand, the Draft White Paper had argued for a comprehensive real-income tax base, including indexation of capital gains and losses, depreciation, interest income and expense, and losses. This argument must be seen in the light of the fact that inflation at the time was around 8% annually. However, the lack of precedents in other countries and the feared practical problems with measuring real interest meant the comprehensive real-income base received little political support. On the other hand, it was seen as a reasonable sugar-coating for the capital-gains-tax pill that only real capital gains represented an increase in effective purchasing capacity and that, therefore, nominal gains should be deflated by the readily available consumer price index. Government concerns about revenue losses and potential tax-avoidance schemes lay behind arguments to allow only nominal capital losses as a deduction and to quarantine nominal capital losses as deductions only against real capital gains. In the end, the proponents of, and opponents to, the introduction of capital gains taxation were perceived to have had partial wins and losses through the adoption of the compromise that permitted adjustments for inflation on measured net taxable gains.

In 1985 there was a debate about the rate of capital gains taxation. Proposals included a flat rate and both the full and partial inclusion of capital gains in personal, business, or fund incomes at the appropriate statutory marginal income tax rate. In the end, the capital gains tax was applied at statutory marginal income-tax rates, except for the application of an averaging provision under which only one-fifth of a net capital gain was used to assess the marginal tax rate, which was then applied to all of the net capital gain. The use of the marginal income-tax rates was motivated by the consideration that, in combination with the taxation of real capital gains, the distorting effects of inflation were minimized and vertical equity was seen to be served.

In sum, from September 1985 onward, capital gains taxes were applied to a tax base consisting of

- assets acquired after September 1985 (except-owner occupied homes and personal chattels);

- realized gains, with death not being deemed a realization;

- nominal gains for assets held for less than 12 months;

- real gains for assets held for more than 12 months, with acquisition costs and subsequent capital costs indexed according to quarterly movements in the general consumer price index;

- nominal losses deductible against real capital gains.

The resultant base was taxable at the appropriate tax entity's marginal tax rate, with the exception of an averaging provision for individuals.

Effects of capital gains taxation, 1985-1999

The Australian experience with its capital gains tax involving the use of indexation can be considered in terms of its effects on revenue, equity, efficiency, and compliance costs.

Revenue

The new capital gains tax was expected to raise more revenue directly and indirectly by eliminating some opportunities for avoiding taxes. Examples of indirect revenue gains included higher income-tax collections on dividend income, which could no longer be reinvested to achieve untaxed capital gains. They also included higher income-tax collections on wage income from the self-employed, who no longer could reinvest it or distribute it through share ownership schemes for employees. No estimates of the additional revenues via these and other indirect effects have been made and reported.

Estimates of the additional direct revenue collection from the capital gains tax, made at the time it was put into effect, were put at a very low $5 millions in the first year, rising to $25 millions in the fifth year (Keating 1985). These low revenue estimates reflect primarily the grandfather clauses by which only gains on assets acquired after September 1985 were taxable and, in part, the expected effects of indexation. In fact, these revenue estimates proved to be extremely conservative (figure 1). Table 1 shows that in 1996/1997 some $2.1 billions were collected in capital gains tax, 2.3% of total income tax receipts or about 0.4% of GDP. Just over $0.8 billion was collected from individual taxpayers, with 7.0% of individuals paying some capital gains tax. Companies paid $0.7 billion capital gains taxes and funds (mostly superannuation but also life and general insurance) paid $0.6 billion. These data suggest that capital gains tax revenues are a small share of total income-tax receipts or of GDP. However, the value and relative size of the capital gains tax revenues may be expected to grow as the effects of the grandfather clauses concessions diminish still further. Even though the revenue of $2.1 billions from capital gains tax is small, its replacement would require a sizeable general income-tax surcharge or increase in indirect tax rates.

Some indication of the sources of taxable capital gains is provided in table 2. For individuals, gains from the sale of shares, trust distributions, and real estate are quantitatively the most important

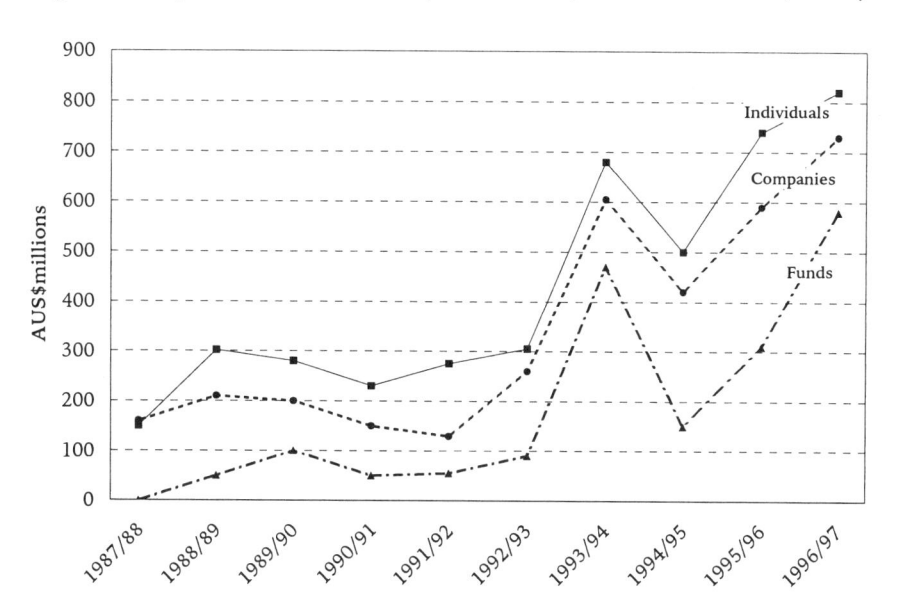

Figure 1: Capital Gains Tax Paid, Australia (1987/1988–1996/1997)

Source: Australian Taxation Office 1998: figure 12.1.

Table 1: Payment of capital gains tax in Australia (1996/1997)

	Individuals	Companies	Funds	Total
Share of taxpayers with taxable capital gains (%)	7.0	4.6	25.6	
Taxable capital gains ($m)	2,899	2,717	3,870	9,486
Capital gains tax paid ($m)	823	729	582	2,134

Source: Australian Taxation Office 1998: tables 12.1 and 12.3.

Companies and especially funds derive most of their capital gains from several different types of property holdings.

Available data shown in table 3 indicate that the capital gains tax has a highly progressive, first-round incidence for individual taxpayers.[3] On average 7% of individual taxpayers pay some capital gains tax but only 5.2% with taxable incomes of less than $20,7000 do so while 21.8% with incomes above $100,000 pay the tax. Data for 1998 from the Australian Tax Office concerning the receipt of dividends by the level of personal income also imply that the first-round incidence of capital gains taxation paid by companies is progressive.

The initial incidence of capital gains taxes paid by funds may be close to a proportional tax in its incidence. This conclusion is based on the fact that compulsory superannuation exists for all but the very low wage earners and there is a flat 15% tax rate on fund earnings including capital gains. In sum, the available evidence suggests strongly that the first-round incidence of capital gains taxation is progressive for individuals, companies and trust funds.

The first round (or statutory) incidence of capital gains tax payments will be equal to the final round (or economic) incidence if the tax does not change the pre-tax rates of return on investment. It is well known that Australia is a small country, which is highly integrated into the global capital markets, has few government re-

Table 2: Sources of capital gains in Australia (1996/1997)

Source of Capital Gain	Proportion of Total Capital Gain (%)		
	Individuals	Companies	Funds
Shares	38.2	24.7	19.2
Trust distributions	19.9	2.7	1.5
Real estate	13.0	2.5	0.3
Other*	11.6	26.7	23.0
More than one of the above	17.3	43.4	55.9

* Includes plant and equipment, personal use assets, goodwill on sale of business, and not stated.
Source: Australian Taxation Office 1998: tables 12.3, 12.4, and 12.5.

Table 3: Distribution of individual taxpayers with capital gains inAustralia (1996/1997)

Taxable income ($ per year)	All taxpayers (#)	Taxpayers with capital gains	
		(#)	(%)
0–20,699	2,887,472	151,504	5.2
20,700–37,999	3,211,422	199,848	6.2
38,000–49,999	1,163,857	97,891	8.3
50,000–99,999	899,300	102,891	12.1
100,000+	127,558	27,862	21.8
TOTAL	8,239,609	579,183	7.0

Source: Australian Taxation Office 1998: table 12.2.

strictions on international capital flows, is a net importer of foreign savings, and has a pervasive system of tax credits for foreign investors. As a result, domestic, risk-adjusted pre-tax rates of return tend to equal such rates in the rest of the world. Under these conditions, the capital gains tax does not change rates of return and the tax unambiguously falls on the domestic owners of the capital.

Table 3 shows that less than 10% of low-income and middle-income taxpayers and around 22% of taxpayers with very high incomes pay capital gains tax. These facts suggest that the capital gains tax has improved considerably horizontal equity on the basis of the comprehensive income benchmark for equity.

It is difficult to assess what effects the introduction of capital gains taxation in 1985 has had on tax neutrality and on efficiency, particularly with respect to the aggregate levels and composition of domestic saving and investment. These difficulties are due to the fact that different tax systems and other concessions affected effective tax rates on savings and investment before and after 1985. Against the benchmark of a comprehensive income tax, the introduction of the capital gains tax was an improvement but it is still distortionary because it is not based on the accrual of gains but on their realization.

Another problem arises in the case of highly levered property investments, which are allowed to deduct from income all nominal debit interest expenses. As Pender and Ross (1993) have argued, in the presence of inflation—even at today's low rates of 2% to 3% but more so at the 8% rate of the 1980s—the inflation adjustment of nominal capital gains results in very low or even negative effective tax rates. In addition, the fact that the capital gains tax is applied only to realized gains at time of sale or gift provides an incentive to lock-in ownership patterns, which involves efficiency losses.

On the other hand, a large proportion of Australian investments is treated as part of the consumption-tax base rather than of the income-tax base. This treatment is applied to owner-occupied homes, about 40% of Australian fixed capital investment, and the increasingly more important items of business investment in research and development and, especially, human capital. Against a consumption-base benchmark, the introduction of capital gains taxation, even with its concessions, introduced too high a level of taxation and associated inefficiencies.

To date, no one has studied the extent to which the 1985 capital gains tax has affected efficiency. Pender and Ross (1993) have shown that the package of 1985 tax changes, including capital gains, the imputation system for companies, superannuation tax changes, and tax rate schedule changes have reduced the variance of effective marginal tax rates on different saving and investment options. However, these findings do not imply that the tax system has become more neutral. To establish this fact it will be necessary to employ computable general equilibrium models and consensus estimates of relevant savings and investment elasticities, a task that is unlikely to be undertaken in the foreseeable future.

There is a high cost of administering the complex income and capital gains tax system of Australia. Many individuals, companies, and funds seek extensive professional tax advice. Evans et al. (1997) have estimated social compliance costs to be 5.6% of revenue from individuals and 15.8% of revenue collected from companies. This study did not estimate compliance costs for the capital gains component alone, presumably because of a lack of relevant basic data. Important costs incurred by the payers of capital gains taxes involve the recording of capital cost items eligible for deduction and of the value of capital items at the time of acquisition and sale. Waincymer (1993), for example, documents the many areas of uncertainty and difficulty in the measurement of net taxable capital gains.

The indexing of capital gains for inflation to determine real capital gains is a trivial and low-cost exercise once the data on acquisition costs and sales values are known. The Australian Taxation Office provides taxpayers with a table of the general consumer price index along with instructions on how it has to be used. For this reason, high compliance costs associated with the measurement of real capital gains as opposed to nominal capital gains has not been a part of any discussions about changes to the Australian system of capital gains taxation.

Changes in 1999

The *Review of Business Taxation* (Ralph et al. 1999) of July 1999 recommended the phasing out of indexation for the measurement of capital gains for taxation, along with partial exclusion of gains from taxation and the cessation of averaging provisions. These proposals were accepted by the government for implementation as of October 1999.

Under the new provisions, the indexation of capital gains was frozen at the end of the September quarter, 1999 and in the future nominal rather than real capital gains became taxable. The indexation was replaced by the provision that 50% of nominal gains for individual taxpayers and 33.3% for superannuation funds were deducted from nominal gains and the remainder was taxable at the appropriate marginal rate of taxation. Companies did not receive such a concession and all of their nominal capital gains were taxable.

Other measures in the package of capital gains tax reforms were the scrapping of the averaging provisions, a zero tax rate on capital assets held by small business proprietors for more than 15 years, script-for-script rollover-takeover relief, and a zero rate for non-resident exempt investors. The change in the mix of concessions and the projected increase in the turnover of assets subject to capital gains taxation were estimated to be approximately revenue neutral.

Stated reasons for the 1999 changes to the taxation of capital gains included improving the rewards for risk and innovation, a better allocation of the nation's resources, improved equity, and greater conformity with the taxation of capital gains in other countries, all within the constraint of a revenue neutral package. To quote the *Review*:

> The Review's recommendations for capital gains taxation are designed to enliven and invigorate the Australian equities markets, to stimulate greater participation by individuals, and to achieve a better allocation of the nation's capital resources. (Ralph et al. 1999: 598).

> Though indexation provides a significant reduction in effective rate for many taxpayers, this is probably not well recognized, especially among foreign investors. Indeed the perception has been that the Australian tax system imposes tax at full income tax rates. Such perceptions are not easily corrected and a change in the form of concession or something more akin to the types of concessions available abroad would, in the Review's judgement, be more effective in attracting investors to Australian assets. (Ralph et al. 1999: 600).

Australia's averaging provisions were identified early as contributing little to those aims while reducing revenue substantially ... This (practice) results in considerable inequity. (Ralph et al. 1999: 599).

Very few quantitative or qualitative arguments were provided to support the claims that the new tax code would result in more and better quality investments and greater equity.

Effects of 1999 changes

Some understanding of the effects upon revenue, efficiency, and equity of the changes to capital gains taxation can be obtained from comparing concessions provided before and after the 1999 reforms. The real capital gains system of the 1985 to 1999 period applied the statutory income rate, t, to the real capital gain measured as the gross asset price increase, g, less the increase in the CPI, p. That is, revenue collected is given by

$$t(g-p) \tag{1}$$

By contrast, under the system after 1999, a proportion z, where $z = 0.5$ for individuals and $z = 0.67$ for superannuation funds, of the gross asset price increase, g, is taxed at the statutory income tax rate, t, so that revenue collected is

$$t\,z\,g \tag{2}$$

Equating (1) and (2) for individuals with $z = 0.5$, the pre-1999 and the post-1999 systems collect the same revenue and have the same effective tax rates, if the asset-price growth rate is double the inflation rate. Or, the new system collects more capital gains tax, if the inflation rate accounts for more than a half of the growth rate of asset prices. For superannuation funds, with $z = 0.67$, the new system collects less capital gains tax if the nominal asset growth rate is at least treble the inflation rate.

From the point of view of individual investors, the new taxation rules lower the effective tax rate on capital gains relative to that under the preceding regime, if during the holding period of an asset, the cumulative rate of inflation is less than 50% of the cumulative nominal increase in the asset value. Investors lose if inflation accounts for greater than 50% of the gain. This fact implies that the possible future return of high inflation rates will result in higher government revenues, effective tax rates, and more serious economic distortions than did the pre-1999 system.

Then, the new capital gains tax system favours investment options with relatively large gains over those with small gains and it favours investment in assets earning capital gains in periods of low inflation versus periods of moderate and high inflation. The tax preference for risky investments with large potential gains might be interpreted as an incentive for innovation in, say, information technology and biotechnology ventures rather than in more conservative ventures like real estate and retailing companies. Whether there are market-failure arguments for such tax biases is undeveloped in the *Review* and uncertain more generally.

In justification of the new tax rule, the *Review* argued that investors base their decisions to buy and sell only, or primarily, on the nominal rate of taxation for capital gains. Since, under the new rules, this rate effectively is halved for individuals (and reduced by one third for superannuation funds), the *Review* suggests that investors will consider the new rules as having produced a lower rate and that, therefore, it will reduce the magnitude of the lock-in effect and other inefficiencies that accompany the capital gains tax. I view this position as highly tenuous since it assumes that investors' motives are irrational when it comes to weighting the tax implications of their decisions. The best that can be said about the new rules is that they lower the effective rate of taxation if inflation rates remain low and do not exceed 50% of the nominal capital gain over the expected holding period for the majority of investors.

Table 4 shows the projected static and dynamic effects of the 1999 reforms on capital gains tax revenues in 2001/2002 and 2004/2005 from individuals, superannuation funds, and other entities. For individuals and superannuation funds, the static effects are shown in the first three lines of each section. Under the assumption that investors do not change their behaviour, these three lines show the change in revenue due to the freezing of indexation, the abolishment of averaging, and the exclusion of a portion of capital gains from taxation (50% for individuals and 33.3% for superannuation funds). The dynamic effects of the reforms are shown in the fourth

Table 4: Projected revenue gains and losses of 1999 capital gains tax reforms, Australia (2001/2002 and 2004/2005) ($millions)

	2001/2002	2004/2005
Individuals		
Freezing indexation (static)	230	490
Abolishing averaging (static)	290	390
50% exclusion (static)	−820	−1,180
Revenue from extra realizations	530	400
Net Effect	230	100
Superannuation Funds		
Freezing indexation (static)	250	520
33.3% exclusion (static)	−350	−620
Revenue from extra realizations	50	30
Net Effect	−50	−70
Other Entities		
Freezing indexation (static)	40	70

A "−" denotes a revenue loss. Static assumes no quantity behavioural references. Key assumptions include: 8% growth in tax base to 2002/2003, then 6%; 2.5% inflation. Extra realizations assumes an elasticity of 1.7 with respect to the effective tax rate for 2001/2002 and then 0.9 for 2004/2005.
Source: Ralph et al. (1999): table 24.10

line of the sections for individuals and superannuation funds. They represent estimates of changes in revenues made under the assumption that the new tax rules induce investors to turn over their asset holdings more frequently.

Table 4 shows that the freezing of indexation is estimated to cost revenue of about $500 million in 2001/2002 and over $1 billion by 2004/2005. These estimates assume a 2.5% inflation rate, which is the mid-point of the Reserve Bank's inflation target band. The abolition of averaging is projected to increase revenue by $290 million in 2001/2002 and $390 million in 2004/2005. Projected revenue losses of the exclusion of a portion of nominal capital gains from taxation are estimated to reduce revenue by $1,170 million in

2001/2002 and $1,800 million in 2004/2005. On this static scenario assessment, individuals and superannuation funds would pay less capital gains tax, or the effective capital gains tax rate falls. Companies are projected to pay more capital gains tax.

The revenue projections in table 4 include also an increase in revenue from projected extra realizations, or more frequent sales, of property subject to capital gains taxation.[5] Higher revenue gains of $580 million for 2001/2002 compared to $430 million for 2004/2005 follow from the assumption of an initial surge and subsequent slowdown in such realizations. Combining the static and dynamic effects results in projected aggregate capital gains tax revenue to be increased by a small amount.

The redistributional effects of the 1999 capital gains tax reforms are likely to be mixed. Removal of the averaging provisions was promoted by the *Review* to end some tax avoidance schemes used by the better off, thereby improving vertical and horizontal equity. But, at the same time, some taxpayers with low or medium incomes will also be losers if they have infrequent "lumpy" capital gains and are not involved in sophisticated tax-avoidance schemes. Following from the tax-payment comparisons shown in equations (1) and (2) above, the reforms will lower tax burdens for those investing in high-return and more risky property investments relative to those with investments in assets that are less risky and realize lower average capital gains. It is debatable that these patterns of tax redistribution accord with general equity goals.

Conclusions

From 1985 to 1999, Australian income taxation included the taxation of real capital gains made on property held for more than 12 months. The adjustment from nominal to real gains was accomplished through deflation of the nominal gains using the quarterly general consumer price index. However, only nominal capital losses were deductible, and proposals in the 1985 Draft White Paper for a comprehensive real income-tax base received little political support. By the 1990s, when the effects of grandfather clauses began to wane, the capital gains tax had become a useful but relatively small revenue earner. Its incidence was progressive. However, it is not clear whether the capital gains tax improved or worsened tax neutrality and efficiency since Australia's taxation base rests partly on consumption and partly on income.

In 1999, following recommendations of the Review of Business Taxation, the indexation of capital gains was frozen. The new taxation of nominal gains, combined with the termination of existing averaging provisions, would have resulted in large revenue gains. To compensate for these gains, the new rules allowed individual taxpayers to exclude 50% of their nominal gains from taxable income. For superannuation funds, the exclusion rates was set at 33.3%. Companies had to pay capital gains on the full amount of their nominal gains.

The stated objectives of these reforms of the capital gains tax were to encourage innovation, promote domestic and overseas investment in Australian business, and achieve greater equity. It is not clear that these objectives of the reform will be achieved since their attainment depends on questionable assumptions about the rationality of investors, especially that they do not understand the benefits of indexing and put great weight on the fact that only one half of their nominal capital gains are taxable.

In fact, the practical administration and compliance costs of indexing capital gains in Australia were trivial, especially relative to the formidable work and cost involved in measuring nominal capital gains by considering the cost of purchases initially and during the holding period in relation to the realized value of the assets. It required very little effort to apply to these nominal gains the quarterly values of the consumer price index, which the tax authorities provided free of charge to all taxpayers in printed as well as electronic form.

Notes

1 Formally, the static allocative efficiency costs, or deadweight costs, of taxation of a particular economic activity are given by $DW\,C/R = n\varepsilon\,t^2/(n + \varepsilon)$, where DWC is the deadweight cost, R is revenue of the activity (or price × quantity), n is the (absolute) elasticity of demand, ε is the elasticity of supply, and t is the proportional tax rate as a share of price. Now, the deadweight cost rises more than proportionally with increases in the tax rate; for activities with similar supply and demand elasticities, a similar tax rate across activities minimizes deadweight costs; and the deadweight loss is greater the more elastic is demand or supply. In addition to the static allocative efficiency costs of taxation, there may be costs of lobbying to reduce particular taxes or to retain tax concessions and preferences.

2 The chapters by Grubel, Oliver, and Yuen and Hsu provide examples of some of the tax-avoidance arrangements.

3 Grubel (2000) argues that the data in table 3 provide a misleading picture of the vertical-equity effects of capital gains taxation on the grounds that the lumpy and infrequent payment of capital gains tax by individuals artificially inflates the number of high-income taxpayers paying capital gains tax. This point is valid in the Canadian context but in Australia the effect is mitigated by the existing averaging procedures. Ralph et al. (1999) argue that income splitting among family members and strategic choosing of when to take capital gains are used as tax avoidance by many high-income taxpayers. Finally, in Australia only 38.5% of capital gains tax revenue is paid by individuals, with the rest paid by companies and funds on behalf of their individual owners.

4 See note 1 for a more formal statement of the reasoning behind these arguments.

5 The projected gains of higher rates of turnover of assets subject to capital gains seems to take account of the effect of the exclusion conditions lowering the effective tax rate, but it ignores the increase in effective tax rates associated with removal of indexation and averaging. That is, the projected dynamic revenue efficiency gains seem to be overly optimistic.

References

Australian Taxation Office (1998). *Taxation Statistics 1996-97*. Canberra: AusInfo.

Draft White Paper (1985). *Reform of the Australian Tax System*. Canberra: AGPS.

Evans, C., K. Ritchie, B. Tran-Nam, and M. Walpole (1997). *A Report into Taxpayer Costs of Compliance*. Canberra: AGPS.

Grubel, H. (2000). *Unlocking Canadian Capital: The Case for Capital Gains Tax Reform*. Vancouver, BC: The Fraser Institute.

Keating, P. (1985). *Reform of the Australian Taxation System*. Canberra: AGPS.

Pender, H., and S. Ross (1993). *Income Tax and Asset Choice in Australia*. EPAC Research Paper No. 3. Canberra: AGPS.

Ralph, J., R. Allert, and R. Joss (1999). *Review of Business Taxation: Report*. Canberra: AGPS.

Waincymer, J. (1993). *Australian Income Tax: Principles and Policy* (2nd ed.). Sydney: Butterworths.

Capital gains taxation in Ireland

MOORE MACDOWELL

In considering the design and operation of a capital gains tax the first issue to be addressed is the rationale for the introduction of the tax in the first place. In general, a capital gains tax is presumed to be either part of a regime of capital or wealth taxation, or an element in the taxation of income, or both. In Ireland's case, the tax was formally introduced as part of a package of capital taxes, although closer analysis suggests that, in fact, it was seen as providing an additional element in the income-tax code.

Prior to the mid-1970s, there was no specific tax on capital gains in Ireland. Capital taxes were confined in the main to inheritance duties. These, in turn, were watered down by provisions affecting agricultural land (at the time, agriculture accounted for about 30% of employment and 25% of economic activity). The only other form of capital taxation was taxation of real estate by local authorities, an annual tax on a base supposed to reflect rental value. This rental value had originally been estimated in the middle of

---

The author wishes to acknowledge the great help and critical comments on an earlier draft, which were provided by Michael O'Grady of the Revenue Commissioners in Dublin Castle. Notes will be found on pages 166–67.

the nineteenth century in a survey of real state values, and by the late twentieth century was full of anomalies and inequitable treatment of similar properties. This tax was referred to as "rates," and was levied as a tax of so many pounds per pound of rateable value (the notional rental value of the property). It applied to residential, commercial, and industrial property and, to a lesser extent, to agricultural land. During the 1970s, political competition led to a program of elimination of rates on domestic housing.

A combination of immediate fiscal problems arising from the first oil shock and the ideological leanings of a centre-left coalition in office from 1973 to 1977 resulted in a radical departure in the field of taxation in 1974. This took the form of a package of capital taxes.

The Government published a White Paper in February of that year in which it outlined the case for the introduction of a package of three kinds of capital taxes: first, capital gains tax proper (*Capital Taxation* 1974); second a general wealth tax; and, third, a capital acquisitions tax, which covered inheritance, gifts and other transfers.

The initial motivation cited by the Government was to replace and reduce large elements of the existing taxation of wealth passing at death under Estate Duty. The pressure for this arose from the substantial increase in the value of land holdings in real terms after Ireland entered the European Economic Community.

The standard equity arguments for having capital taxation as well as income taxation were used to justify these new taxes: "Income, in the commonly accepted sense of the term, is not the sole measure of comparative circumstances ... It is clear, therefore, that income taxation is inadequate on its own if the tax structure is designed to meet the test of taxable capacity" (*Capital Taxation* 1974: 23). Apart from a throwaway remark about encouraging the efficient use of capital assets by taxing them, the issue of the efficiency effect of these taxes was simply not addressed in the White Paper.

The public's response to the Government's proposals was mixed. The main emphasis of the ensuing debate was on the wealth tax and the sides taken were entirely predictable. The Opposition and the financial press were extremely hostile to the proposed wealth tax. The response from disinterested bodies was less critical but even there concern was expressed about details of the package. In relation to the capital gain tax it was immediately pointed out that the absence of indexation implied an effective rate of taxation that could exceed 100% (NESC 1974: 7). It was also pointed out that restricting the tax to realized gains on disposal implied a lock-in effect (NESC 1974: 8). The question of lock-in had not even been addressed in the White Paper, nor had the inflation problem.

The wealth tax was subsequently repealed but the capital gains tax was retained, and the capital acquisitions tax was used to replace inheritance taxation.

The history of capital gains taxation in Ireland

The introductory phase[1]

Prior to the introduction of capital gains tax under Ireland's schedular income-tax system,[2] capital gains were taxable as income to the extent that they could be treated as income as defined by law. By and large, capital gains were not taxable unless an individual lived by trading in assets. In corporate hands, similarly, capital gains would be liable to corporate profits tax to the extent that they could be treated as profits. As a result of high marginal tax rates on income, the tax increased the incentive to re-structure the legal basis of accruals so as to transform taxable income or profits into non-taxable capital gains. Several cases of substantial tax avoidance based on this maneuver became public.

Whatever may have been the rhetoric about taxing wealth, the reality was that the principal effect of the capital gains tax was to supplement the conventional income tax. This effect was achieved by bringing an untaxed form of income into the tax net, albeit at a significantly lower marginal rate than that charged on personal income at the time. It should, therefore, be viewed as an attempt to move towards a more complete system of income taxation, as was proposed by Simons, who had argued that capital gains and income are equivalent because they affect equally the ability of individuals to consume without affecting net worth.

The provisions governing the capital gains tax in Ireland introduced in the middle 1970s were very much in the mainstream of the OECD. At that time and for a long time thereafter, many OECD countries did not have a specific capital gains tax in place. Instead, many imposed taxes on realized capital gains under the various income tax codes. In this sense, the detailed provisions of the Irish tax code were very similar to those in effect in other countries of the OECD (cf. Sanford 1988: 121–54).

The grounding legislation in Ireland is the Capital Gains Tax Act, 1975, which became law in August of that year. It applied capital gains from the beginning of the fiscal year 1974/1975 or, more precisely, to gains realized after April 6, 1974. The tax was imposed on realized rather than accrued gains arising from the sale or disposal of a taxable asset.

Chargeable gain

For tax purposes, a gain is equal to the actual or, in the case of a transfer, notional price of the asset obtained on disposal minus the sum of its purchase price adjusted for certain costs and certain allowable deductions. The gain is based on the asset price after April 6, 1974. For assets held before that date, the gain is the smaller of the difference between the realization value and the value at purchase (including certain costs) or the value as of April 1974. Deductions include improvement expenditure and transactions costs. They do not include the costs of holding assets, like interest, insurance, and payments to asset managers. It is therefore clear that the tax is based on the realized increase in the market value of the asset, not on the increase in the asset holders' net wealth arising from the increase in the value of the asset. This aspect of the tax will be considered in a later section of this chapter.

Disposal and realization

For the purposes of a charge under the capital gains tax, a disposal or realization takes place whenever (with limited exceptions) the owner of an asset transfers it to another individual. This applies to gifts as well as to sales. On death, assets are taxed in the hands of the recipients and not of the transferor. Importantly, Irish capital gains tax law has never regarded the transfer of property at death as a disposal or realization subject to tax. In effect, all capital gains tax liabilities were expunged at death.

Furthermore, the recipients of assets through inheritance or bequest are considered to acquire the assets at their market value, not at the cost to the deceased. Capital acquisitions tax was (and is) levied on acquisitions in excess of threshold values. These refer to lifetime acquisitions. An individual is entitled to receive a cumulative total limited by the threshold over his lifetime. The threshold values vary according to the relation of the recipient to the transferor. At a time when the thresholds for capital acquisitions taxation were quite low, the tax rate was 40% and there was a 2% probate tax, this regulation did not have much impact on property disposition. However, higher thresholds in recent years had the effect of enhancing lock-in effects.

In principle, the broad definition of a disposal leaves open the possibility of double taxation on a transfer by gift. This is so because the capital gains tax is applied upon a sale and purchase. However, the capital gains tax paid by the donor is credited against the capital gains tax liability of the recipient. The gift is taxed at its nominal value for the purposes of capital gains taxation, while the donor pays CGT on the amount transferred. For example, if A transfers £100,000 to B and attracts a tax liability of £15,000 on this disposal or realization, B's tax liability is based on the entire £100,000. In other words, in this example the recipient is liable for money that he did not receive and, in effect, pays a tax on a tax already paid. However, this provision is made less onerous by the fact that, if the capital gains taxes are less than the charges under the capital acquisition charge, the former is credited against the latter liability. In practice, this provision means that a gift is taxed at the higher of the effective rates applicable to the donor or recipient, be it the capital gains tax or the capital acquisition tax. At present, the rates on the two taxes are the same and the provision is not important but this has not always been the case.

In most cases, disposals to the state, certain charities, and transfers between spouses are exempt from capital gains taxation. In the case of "accidental" disposal arising, for example, from a compulsory purchase order for land under eminent domain powers or a receipt of insurance compensation for the damage or destruction of an insured asset, roll-over relief prevents the accrual of capital gains tax obligations provided certain conditions are met.

Tax base: asset value enhancement

From the start, the capital gains tax was very much a selective tax on asset-value enhancement. A wide and economically significant range of wealth assets were excluded in part or whole from liability to the tax on any increase in value. For example, normally depreciable assets are valued at their purchase price minus any depreciation. This rule does not apply to assets held as business equipment. Principal private residences (one per person) remain excluded from the capital gains tax.[3] The Government also exempted most liabilities of public sector financial intermediaries from the tax, no doubt reflecting the contemporary preoccupation of the authorities with the costs involved in financing the very high annual Exchequer borrowing requirement. Pension funds were accorded favorable treatment in terms of realizations and in terms of payments to beneficiaries.

Social concerns were also addressed by limits on capital gains taxes payable on the transfer of small family farms and businesses within the family. Gains accruing from the increase in the value of standing timber were exempt. Charities and certain public bodies were exempt from paying taxes on gains arising from disposals.

Where a wealth-holder sold an asset and invested the proceeds in another asset (i.e., could be said to be changing the composition of his portfolio rather than partly or wholly liquidating it), and the sale was exempt from CGT it was said to be covered by "rollover relief." Rollover relief was provided for the disposals of assets and re-investment of the proceeds within businesses. However, rollover relief is not available for financial portfolio adjustments by individuals. Instead, each disposal of an asset in a financial portfolio has to be treated as a stand-alone realization and all such disposals have to be aggregated within the relevant tax year to arrive at a figure for taxable gain. Realized losses can be used to reduce taxable gains. This provision leads to some "bed and breakfast" transactions at the end of financial accounting periods as portfolio holders have an incentive to "realize" losses on assets that they intend to hold onto in the longer term. "Bed and breakfast" is a term used to cover paper transactions designed to establish a particular tax liability position. For example, an asset holder might sell shares that had declined in value to establish a loss that could offset a chargeable gain and immediately re-purchase the same number of shares.

The present rules of capital gains taxation applied to the management of portfolios imply that those that are managed actively are taxed on approximately an accrual basis. On the other hand, portfolios that are not managed are taxed only when they are partly or wholly liquidated. As a result, the present system provides an implicit subsidy to passive portfolio management.

When financial assets are held through approved intermediaries, however, rollover relief is implicitly available because the gains are not chargeable to capital gains tax. However, losses in such funds cannot offset gains realized on other assets. The approved institutions are in the main pension funds and the like but other investment intermediaries can also operate funds that, in effect, defer any charge on net gains until the maturity of the individual's holding in the fund.

Further amendments to the Capital Gains Tax code and implementation procedures

When capital gains taxation was introduced the rate was 26%. This rate was about one third of the highest marginal personal income tax rate then in force. For small gains, individuals had an option of having the gain treated as income on the basis of a zero rate on a first tranche. Any gains above that tranche in a given year were subject a 50% rate of taxation. This fact implies that from the beginning the tax regime treated capital gains as a separately taxable form of income. In other words, the tax code acknowledged that the tax base was fungible. Corporations were able to have capital gains taxed under the Corporations Profits Tax so that they owed the same as if the gains had been imposed at the rate of the capital gains tax.

The high inflation rates of the 1970s resulted in high capital gains taxes on assets held for long periods. In response to protest over this unfair tax, some major changes in the original capital gains tax regime were introduced. The first of these, introduced in 1978, was an inflation-adjustment mechanism designed to limit the tax liability to changes in the real rather than the monetary value of assets. This adjustment took the form of what was termed an "inflation multiplier," which was simply the percentage change in the Consumer Price Index in the year up to the beginning of the current financial year beginning on April 6. In practice, the procedure requires an increase in the purchase value of assets by the rate of inflation. The resultant adjusted purchase value is subtracted from the disposal value to arrive at the taxable capital gain. Since the income tax code made no allowance for inflation in determining a person's tax liability on a nominal income, this adjustment marked a further substantial departure from the basic concept that the capital gains tax is a form of income that escaped the income tax.

The 1978 Finance Act also introduced differential tax treatments depending on the length of time an asset had been held. This arrangement can be seen as a form of inflation relief, which already had been granted through the inflation multiplier provision just discussed. So, why was it considered necessary to add this new provision? The authorities offered the argument that the capital gains tax was a disincentive to long-term, *genuine* investment. Such investment was needed to encourage capital formation, which would relieve Ireland's chronic problem of underemployment and foster structural change needed in the wake of accession to membership in the European Economic Community. On the other hand, accruals of wealth based on mere *speculation* were considered to be a legitimate target of taxation on the grounds of equity. Since assets held for longer time periods were already subject to inflation indexing, the lower rate of taxation for them means that they were over-compensated for inflation.

The standard equity argument for treating long-term gains more favourably than short-term gains arises from the existence of a progressive income-tax structure. Thus, if capital gains are taxed annually, they are likely to be subject to a lower rate than if the annual gains are accumulated and become so large that the taxpayer is pushed into a higher marginal tax rate in the year the gains are realized. In fact, however, this argument could not be used in Ireland because the relevant tax rate, the capital gains tax rate was flat. Except for an annual exemption of £2,000,[4] the marginal rate was the same whatever other income was gained or capital gains realized. There was, therefore, no justification for introducing the holding-period adjustment to rates as introduced in Ireland on the basis of higher rates on larger gains in the year of realization, as would have been the case if the CGT were similar to an income tax with increasing marginal rates.

In the case of small gains, the annual exemption did make a substantial difference. Consider a gain of £20,000 over five years on an asset held for five years. It would give rise to a tax charge on a gain of £18,000, if realized in year 5, but only on a gain of £10,000, if realized in five tranches of £4,000 over five successive years, as £2000 was exempt in each year. Hence, with five realizations of £4,000, 50% of the total gain would be exempt. For smaller gains, therefore, the lock-in effect of Capital Gains Tax was to some extent offset by the annual exemption

The 1978 review of the tax code increased the base rate on capital gains to 30% and introduced rate adjustments reflecting holding periods. This rate applied to *short-term* gains, defined as gains on an asset held for less than three years. If an asset were held for between three and six years before disposal, the rate fell to 25.5%. For each additional three years for which an asset was held, the applicable rate fell by amounts of between 3% and 4.5% until at 21 years any gain was tax-free.

The fiscal crisis of the early 1980s resulted in a sharp increase in the rates of capital gains taxation. Thus, in 1982 gains made within one year of purchase were taxed at 60%. For holding periods of one to three years, the rate was increased to 50% and, for assets held for more than three years, the rate was raised to 40%. In the case of development land, the lower rate was held at 50% and the inflation adjustment was limited to the value of the land prior to its being granted planning permission for development.

The tax rates related to holding periods were adjusted in 1986 and 1990 and the number of periods was reduced to four: less than a year—60%, less than three years—50%, less than six years—35%, and over six years—30%. Reduced rates were temporarily applied to gains on sales of shares in quoted companies in the Smaller Companies Market of the Irish Stock Exchange and to certain tax-sheltered investment schemes.

In 1992, it was found necessary to introduce a capital gains tax shelter for assets sold by owners to a company in their control in return for shares in that company as part of incorporation. For this provision to come into effect, the shares had to be held for at least five years. In effect, the policy provided a form of rollover relief.

In 1994, the capital gains tax was overhauled once again with the introduction of a single 40% rate. In addition, the distinction between short-term and long-term gains was abandoned for most purposes. In order to facilitate incorporation and acquisitions, it was provided that, in some sectors and where assets had been held for 5 years or more, gains on disposals would be taxed at 27%, reduced to 26% in 1997. Problems of rollover relief were also addressed again at this point in order to facilitate the sale and reinvestment of assets in small enterprises.

At the end of 1997, a further major shift in emphasis took place. The capital gains tax rate was reduced to 20%, with a *proviso* that this rate was to be temporary on development land zoned residential: the tax on gains from residential development land is slated to be 60% from 2002. This provision was expressly designed to induce the advanced realization of gains in order to discourage *hoarding* of development land, a practice seen as contributing to a perceived growing housing shortage. Gains on other development land continued to attract a 40% tax. This latter change has introduced the possibility that the capital gains tax could actually be used to avoid income tax rather than complementing or completing it. This result is due to interactions among the capital gains tax and corporations tax on the one hand and the personal income tax at a rate higher than the first two on the other hand.

To take advantage of the different tax treatment, business, trade, or professional firms can incorporate. If profits are retained rather than distributed, they are liable to the corporations tax. There is incomplete allowance for corporation tax paid on profits out of which dividends are paid in computing the shareholder's personal tax liability on his dividend income. This implies double taxation of profits income. As a consequence, the tax code, until recently, penalized incorporation if a small business wished to accumulate capital. The tax charge was reduced by distributing all surplus as income and taxing it as earned income in the hands of the recipient rather than accruing it as retained profit within the firm and then distributing it. In recent years, however, the balance began to swing in the other direction, as the corporation tax was reduced towards a target rate of 12.5% on all profits.[5] From 2001, the first £100,000 profits is taxed at 12.5%. When the capital gains tax was reduced to 20%, the accrual of surplus as profit in a corporation allowed taxpayers to opt for paying the 12.5% corporation rather than the 44% marginal income-tax rate. The lower tax rate could be paid annually until the company is sold. At this point, the owner would pay the capital gains tax due on the retained earnings.

An example helps to illustrate this important point. Consider that £100 is distributed as earned income from the corporation to the owner. This payment attracts a tax and social-security charge of £46. But, if the corporation retains the earnings, there is a tax bill of £12.50 paid by the business, which has an extra £31.50 (£46 minus £12.50) to invest. As a result of this additional investment, the corporation's value increases and gives rise to a capital gain when the owner sells it. The capital gain is taxed at 20%. In sum, without discounting and disregarding the earnings from the corporation's investment of the retained earnings, the tax liability on £100 retained is £12.50 plus 20% × £87.50 = £17.50, which makes for a total of £30. In effect, the reinvestment of the corporate earnings reduces the owner's tax burden to 30% from the 46% payable if the earnings had been distributed. It is clear that these conditions encourage not only the reinvestment of earnings by corporations, they also provide strong incentives for the incorporation of businesses.

To reduce these incentives for the evasion of taxes, the Government introduced a surcharge on some undistributed trading income in "close" companies in the 1999 Budget. More precisely, the surcharge applies to retentions in excess of 50% of profits after tax.

Experiences with the capital gains tax

Initially, the capital gains tax, in contrast to the personal income tax, required self-assessment. Thus, the capital gains tax could only be collected if taxpayers notified the revenue authorities that they had a taxable gain. Employees are supposed to file annual returns, which included reports on capital gains. But, the Revenue authorities did not in practice demand returns from lower-income employees and, hence, did not bother checking these cases for capital gains, presumably under the assumption that most employees have no other income or capital gains. Instead, the Revenue authorities sought returns only from higher earners or earners with multiple sources of income. This category does, in fact, contain most taxpayers with capital gains tax liabilities but without independent sources of information, the potential for evasion by the average taxpayer was very high. The laws applying to corporations are such that there have been few problems with the non-reporting of capital gains.

Since the middle 1990s, however, self-assessment has become the general principle for all personal direct taxes in Ireland, including the capital gains tax. Under self assessment for income tax, all tax-payers making a return of income tax are obliged in this return to make a declaration of asset realizations as part of their income-tax returns. Previously, an income-tax return could be made without declaring capital gains, as the latter involved a separate return.

The shift to self-assessment is generally accepted as having improved compliance, despite apparently creating of room for evasion. The reasons for this are the following. First, the presumption of truthful reporting reduced the quantity of paperwork demanded and improved relations between tax payers (and their advisers) and the Revenue authorities. Secondly, it took place at a time when tax rates were falling. Thirdly, it was accompanied by the introduction of random and statistical anomaly auditing along American lines, with a credible commitment to substantial penalties for evasion (previously penalties had been light and largely negotiable).

When the capital gains tax was first introduced, in its first full year of application it yielded a paltry £400,000 out of a total tax take of over £1.2 billion, or 0.03% of the total (see table 1). This revenue was equivalent to about 0.1% of the yield of the personal income tax. However, from 1978 on, there was a sharp increase in the yield in absolute terms and, by 1980, the yield was equal to 0.6% of the income-tax yield. It is worth noting that this increase in revenue occurred in the wake of the introduction of inflation indexing and differential taxing of short-term and long-term gains in 1978. It appears that these policies reduced tax liabilities on the one hand but encouraged realizations and reporting on the other sufficiently to bring the large increase in revenues. This result is consistent with the effects of changes on rates of capital gains taxation on revenue observed later. In particular, it suggests that within a reasonable range, the lowering of capital gains tax rates increases government revenues from that tax. However, it remains unclear to what extent this result stems from increased realizations, that is, the unlocking of capital, and to what extent from increased compliance.

Between 1983 and 1994, capital gains tax rates were high. Between 1984 and 1987, the yield from the capital gains tax rose from about £9 millions to £13 millions, though it remained more or less static at about 0.2% of total tax receipts and at about 0.46% of the income-tax yield. In the absence of any statistical analysis by the Revenue authorities of the reported realizations, it is not wise to offer strong conclusions as to the impact of the greatly increased rates and the reduced tapering rate for length of ownership imposed in 1983. In addition, it should be noted that during the years from 1983 to 1987 Ireland experienced the deepest and longest recession since the 1950s.

In the later part of the high-tax years, from 1988 to 1994, the average yields were substantially higher than in the earlier, higher-rate years. However, it is unclear to what extent these revenue gains were due to the fact that the economy was pulling sharply out of the recession. It is notable also that the yield was very volatile over these later years, which weakens any argument that rates affect the yield predictably, except perhaps in the short term.

Table 1: Tax receipts by calendar year (£ million), 1975–1997

	Total tax receipts	Capital Acquisitions Tax	Capital gains tax	Income tax	Corporations tax
1997	13,791	89	132	5,208	1,687
1996	12,092	82	84	4,579	1,428
1995	10,885	60	44	4,129	1,148
1994	10,416	59	47	4,098	1,141
1993	9,241	51	27	3,803	953
1992	8,560	33	58	3,414	739
1991	8,003	45	48	3,222	594
1990	7,616	38	28	3,029	475
1989	7,164	29	25	2,831	303
1988	7,068	27	33	3,051	335
1987	6,257	25	13	2,721	256
1986	5,861	21	11	2,416	258
1985	5,353	20	10	2,180	218
1984	5,115	18	9	2,046	210
1983	4,503	15	9	1,701	215
1982	4,014	12	8	1,458	232
1981	3,274	9	6	1,246	200
1980	2,584	8	6	1,013	140
1979	1,991	8	4	732	130
1978	1,709	5	3	604	106
1977	1,445	3	2	523	76
1976	1,222	..	..	461	29
1975	901	–	..	332	27

Source: Revenue Commissioners Annual Reports and Annual Statistics

The yield performance from 1995 to 1997 suggests that lower rates of capital gains taxation and simpler rules can raise revenues from the tax. But again, the performance of stock markets in Ireland and elsewhere plus a rapidly expanding economy with accelerating property prices limit the extent to which the experience can be used to prove that lower tax rates necessarily lead to higher tax revenues.

Compliance was a serious problem until the early 1990s. At that time the tax authorities obtained powers to demand information from auctioneers and stockbrokers about capital gains realized by their clients. This new policy and that of not permitting full self-assessment led to a high variability of yield from year to year. The tax authorities noted that the large revenue increases in some years were due to a number of large settlements. Despite the administrative and compliance problems just discussed, the capital gains tax by the middle 1990s yielded in excess of 1% of the personal conventional income-tax revenues.

Analysis and conclusions

Ireland's experience with the capital gains tax allows insights into the following questions relevant to policy-makers considering reforms of the Canadian capital gains tax system:

(1) the design and effects of indexation;

(2) valuation and compliance issues affecting certain assets;

(3) the question of interest and other costs in financing asset holdings;

(4) the impact of rate changes on yields and disposals;

(5) the treatment of losses;

(6) the differential taxation of short-term and long-term capital gains.

Indexation

Indexation means that the value of a realized asset is deflated by increases in the consumer price index since the time the asset was acquired. The concept and its implementation are simple. Thus, the authorities publish and supply to taxpayers a table of multiplier coefficients, which are used to adjust upwards the value of an asset for the time between its acquisition or purchase and the time it was sold. This process is extremely simple administratively and it is readily understood by taxpayers.

However, I have some reservations about the use of the consumer price index and concerns about the detrimental effects on efficiency that arise from the way in which indexation is applied in Ireland. The consumer price index was until relatively recently calculated quarterly rather than monthly and, as a result, the value of the index used to compute the inflation adjustment was that for February, which was the last quarterly figure in any given fiscal year, which, in Ireland, ends on April 5. As result of using the value for February rather than that for April, the indexation is biased downward during periods of rising prices. This bias can be serious for assets held for a short time but is much less serious for assets held a long time.

The use of the consumer price index is open to some criticism because it measures changes only in consumer prices, including indirect taxes and subsidies. Many economists prefer to use a more inclusive measure of inflation like the GDP deflator to reflect changes in the value of money more accurately. There is no reason why the GDP deflator should not be used except for the evaluation of short-term gains, because of lags in the availability of this statistic. With some effort, the government should be able to overcome this shortcoming.

Valuation and compliance

Problems associated with the valuation of assets give rise to the use of realized rather than accrued values as the basis for capital gains taxation. Establishing the value of assets on the basis of accruals is impossible in the case of goods for which no independent and unquestionable prices are known. This condition exists in the case of art works, most real estate, closely held shares of companies, and similar assets with unique characteristics and thin markets. On the other hand, accrual values could be used for financial assets like shares in publicly quoted companies, and short-term and long-term private-sector and public-sector debt paper. The relative merit of accruals and realization in the valuation of assets was examined in the early 1980s by a government commission in Ireland, which recommended retaining realization.

In the main, compliance to capital gains taxation of real estate and financial assets has not been a problem for the following reasons. Real estate transactions have to be disclosed to the tax authorities in order to ensure certainty of title. Financial transactions originating with companies are subject to commercial laws, which make it very difficult to conceal or even grossly under-report the value of assets. Furthermore, under-reporting by vendors creates a potential excess tax liability at a future date for purchasers.

To help ensure full compliance, the Irish Revenue Department has some other regulations. Stockbrokers can be asked to provide full details of all financial transactions undertaken by residents through stockbrokers. However, brokers do not have to notify the Revenue Department of transactions[6] but merely to offer their records for inspection upon demand by the authorities. There are no published data to reveal the extent to which the authorities demand records but informal inquiries suggest that the major brokers are not all that frequently subject to requests from the Revenue Department to examine their books.

Compliant taxpayers are required to report in the income-tax return all assets acquired or realized during the tax year. This information automatically triggers an assessment, if self-assessment is not forthcoming in later years. Taxpayers are also required to reveal the sources of the funds used to acquire assets. This policy suggests that the main emphasis of compliance is on the creation of a full picture of the asset profile of taxpayers. Such profiles allow the government to encourage compliance, especially since it has the power of audits and the accompanying mandatory revelation and inspection of accounts with financial institutions.

Auctioneers are legally obliged to supply information about sales of antiques, *objets d'art, objets de vertu*, and the like. It is hard to know with any precision how effective these provisions are in reducing evasion. Auctioneers are required to report individual sales valued at more than £15,000 (approximately CDN$27,500). The larger houses unquestionably comply with these requirements but informal contacts in the business suggest that, after the implementation of this requirement in the early 1990s, businesses not subject to the reporting requirement carried out increasing shares of auctions in Ireland. However, this method of evasion appears to have declined in the wake of lower capital gains tax rates and a growing climate of general compliance.

Interest and other costs

The purchase and sale of assets involves costs. Most assets require carrying charges while they are held. Under the existing tax code in Ireland, only some of these costs can be used to increase the costs of acquisition or decrease the value of a realized gain. As a result, the size of capital gains tends to be over-estimated and the capital gains tax is correspondingly unfair. Allowing adjustments to capital gains for these costs incurred would eliminate this lack of fairness.

However, if the capital gains tax is seen as a complement to the income tax, the absence of adjustment of realized gains through the expenditure of interest and insurance is not out of line with the general provisions of Ireland's income-tax code. Over the last decade, this code has steadily reduced the degree to which interest payments can be used to reduce taxable income. Initially, this provision applied only to consumer loans but in recent years it has been applied even to the politically sensitive interest cost of house mortgages. The deductibility of mortgage costs is now limited in amount and it results in less valuable tax credits rather than tax allowances.

The impact of rate changes

The 1997 Budget halved the rate of taxation of realized capital gains from 40% to 20%. The Minister for Finance was heavily criticized at the time for what was seen as a highly regressive change in the tax code. He responded to this criticism by arguing that the lower rate would increase revenues substantially. The data in table 2 suggest that the Minister was right. Revenues did indeed increase by large amounts. The table also shows that the forecasts of the revenue effects of the lower tax rates were far off the mark.

It is important to consider why lower rates of capital gains taxation give rise to higher rather than lower revenues. The main reason usually given is undoubtedly that lower rates increase incentives to realize gains on appreciated assets. This is a short-term effect and arguably goes some way to explain the rapid yield growth in the Irish case. At the lower tax rate, taxpayers retain more money from the sale of their assets, which is then available for reinvestment. The greater rate of realization induced by the lower tax rate reflects the unlocking of capital, which under the higher tax rates would have remained in the original use. The unlocking of capital induced by the lower rate explains a considerable portion of the higher revenues. It should be remembered, however, that a decision

Table 2: Net receipts the capital gains tax, 1995–1999

Calendar year	Net receipts	Excess over Budget estimate
1995	£44.5 m	£13.5 m
1996	£83.7 m	£25.7 m
1997	£132.4 m	£65.4 m
1998	£193.1 m	£89.1 m
1999	£356.2 m	£163.3 m

Source: Revenue Commission data.

to realize gains sooner and more frequently implies advancing the flow of tax receipts to the Exchequer rather than increasing its steady-state level. This implies a temporary rather than a permanent increase in revenues from a rate cut.

However, the unlocking of capital induced by the lower tax rate is also frequently argued to have the additional effect of increasing the efficiency of the use of capital in the country. As a result, labour productivity and economic prosperity are expected to be increased. In the long run, reflecting this, capital gains and opportunities for higher yielding investments grow in response and lead to even more realizations, higher revenues, and greater prosperity in a virtuous cycle. This may result in a permanent, or steady-state, increase in the yield of the tax.

In the Irish case, there is some evidence that suggests that the reduction in the rate of capital gains taxation may not have been responsible for all of the large revenue gains shown in table 2 (see Appendix 1). That said, there is no doubt that the Minster's confidence expressed at Budget time as to the likely yield of capital gains tax was subsequently justified by the yield figures.

The treatment of losses

Under the present tax code, realized losses from the sale of a capital asset may be offset against realized gains in the same tax year. If losses exceed gains in the same year, the losses may be used to reduce the value of capital gains in the preceding or following years. The system thus permits the offset of losses against gains but, importantly, only for gains and losses from the sale of assets and then only during a restricted number of years. These provisions are inconsistent with the principles enunciated in the White Paper of 1975, which had envisioned complete offsets against all types of income and involves the fiscal authorities in sharing portfolio risks with taxpayers.

The incomplete sharing of the risk has important economic consequences in terms of potentially discouraging risky investments, which are essential to technical progress and economic growth. The analysis of the impact of loss-offset provisions on risk taking and its consequences for the riskiness of capital portfolios is complex. Some aspects of this problem in relation to the design of the Irish tax structure are considered in Appendix 2. What is beyond dispute, however, is that there is good reason to believe that incomplete loss offset will discourage risk taking. The policy also reduces the welfare of asset holders since they are induced to select portfolios different from what they would in either the absence of a capital gains tax or the full offset of gains and losses.

Differential treatment of short-term and long-term capital gains.
When Ireland first introduced its capital gains tax, it imposed rates on gains depending on the length of time over which the assets were held. This policy was modeled after one existing in Britain in the early 1960s. Subsequently, these provisions were dropped and the tax was imposed uniformly on all capital gains.

I believe that the adoption of the uniform rates is consistent with the first principle underlying the taxation of capital gains. Such gains allow owners of capital to increase expenditures just as income does. Both should therefore be taxed. Under this principle, it makes no sense to have different rates of taxation dependent upon the duration of the investment that gives rise to the capital gains.

One argument often used to justify the higher taxation of short-term gains is that it discourages speculation. Implicit in this justification is the view that speculation is economically and socially undesirable. This view is held by many, especially those whose interests are damaged by higher prices. However, most economists, including myself, believe that in market economies, speculation plays a beneficial role in the efficient allocation of resources through time. The suppression of speculation through taxation therefore reduces the efficiency of the economy, lowers income, and damages prosperity.

Appendix 1: Some reservations about the impact of the tax rate cut

Table 3 shows that the number of assessments and the total tax due on those assessments did not increase as quickly after the tax cut was put into effect on December 3, 1997 as might have been expected. Under existing accounting rules, gains realized in the year ending April 5, 1998 would incur a tax liability payable November 1998. The change in the tax regime took effect from December 3, 1997 and was not anticipated (in the sense that it took commentators by surprise).

Notice that between 1995/1996 and 1996/1997 the number of assessments (which in each case is the aggregate of realizations of an individual or of a couple) rose by nearly 25% and the tax to be paid rose by nearly 75%. In the following year, towards the end of which the rate cut came into force, the number of assessments rose by 87% while the tax due increased by 46%. In the next year, the number of assessments rose by 11% but the tax due rose by almost 57% (the results for 1998/1999 are preliminary; see note to table 3). That is, the tax yield increased by considerably more than the percentage increase in realizations.

If we analyze these data, the Laffer-type conclusions appear a little weaker than might be thought at first. In the first place, the Revenue Department itself applied health warnings to these fig-

Table 3: Assessments and tax due, 1993/1994 to 1998/1999

Fiscal year	Number of assessments	Net tax payable
1993/1994	5,189	£30.4 m
1994/1995	4,795	£71.9 m
1995/1996	6,360	£75.4 m
1996/1997	7,958	£131.2 m
1997/1998	14,886	£191.5 m
1998/1999	16,529	£300.5 m

Source: Revenue Commission data
Note: the tax due is what is assessed as due, rather than what was paid, and is subject to revision; the number of assessments, especially for 1998/1999, is likely to increase as returns are received and processed.

ures by noting that, in 1994/1995, 1996/1997, 1997/1998, and 1998/1999 (four of the five years), what are described as "significant" increases in net tax payable are partially attributable to assessments raised in a number of individually large settlements. Internal estimates supplied by the Revenue Department suggest that, in the four fiscal years 1995/1996, 1996/1997, 1997/1998 and 1998/1999, the yields of "once-offs" accounted for £22.2 millions, £31.8 millions, £17.6 millions, and £30.0 millions, respectively. The extent, therefore, to which the data may be construed as indicating underlying yield changes has to be open to question. Ignoring this reservation, however, we are still left with further reason for thinking that all is not as rosy as the Minister for Finance appears to believe.

In the first place, we do not know what proportion of the realizations in 1997/1998 took place between December 3 and April 5. If we extrapolate the trend from 1994/1995 to 1996/1997 into 1997/1998, we would have expected an increase in the number of realizations in excess of the exemption limits to have increased by between 25% and 30% in the latter year. That would give a total of between 9,500 and 10,300 (as opposed to the actual number of about 15,000). As an initial estimate, therefore, it appears reasonable to use a figure of about 5,000 assessments as being possibly due to the impact of the rate cut in terms of increased realizations. Even then, however, it should be remembered that an assessment is raised when the value of a realization exceeds the exemption threshold. Hence, the number of assessments can increase because either or both of two factors have an effect: an increase in the number of realizations (or reported realizations) and an increase in the value of realizations. With booming stock and real-property markets, the latter effect cannot be totally discounted.

In the following year (1998/1999), we see a small increase in the number of assessments but a substantial increase in the tax due, despite the tax rate being halved. That can only mean that the value of the average realization reported has increased very significantly. Again, if we extrapolate the trend before 1997, we would get a number of assessments of about 13,000 in 1998/1999 (actual value, 16,500). If we assume the average size of realization is driven by asset values, this would have produced a total for tax due of about £240 millions, or 80% of what was actually assessed. That suggests that a 50% cut in the tax rate between 1996/1997 and 1998/1999 yielded at best something like a 20% increase in the tax yield. Even that number assumes that the increase in the number of assessments reflects an increase in the number of realizations rather than an increase in the average size of realizations.

The classic supply side argument about self-financing tax cuts cannot be supported by a simple reference to the change in the yield level after the rate cut at the end of 1997. The evidence, however, does point to the existence of some such effect, even if a good deal smaller than apologists claimed.

Appendix 2: Loss offset and risk taking

If we start from a position of a zero tax and an assumed optimal portfolio composition, a change in that composition arising from reaction to taxation constitutes a dead-weight loss flowing from the tax.[7] The impact of varying degrees of loss offset on portfolio composition as determined by acceptance of risk is dependent on assumptions about the behaviour of individuals with respect to risk. In the classic analysis, which treats portfolio variance as a risk measure (and implicitly assumes a quadratic utility function, with its limitations), it is possible, starting from a zero tax to identify two rates of tax,[8] $t = 0$ and $t = t^* > 0$, for which the risk characteristic of the portfolio is the same. The implication of this is that, for usual assumptions as to the utility function of the wealth holder, an increase from zero in the tax rate will result, at first, in a rise and, subsequently, a fall in the chosen value for the portfolio risk parameter. From a *high* value for the rate at which the tax is applied, a reduction in the tax rate will be expected to increase the risk parameter but continued reductions will lead to an eventual fall in the risk parameter. For small changes in the rate of taxation, it has to be accepted that the net effect on risk-taking is a matter for empirical investigation under zero, or less than full-loss offset. Incomplete loss offset, then, has deadweight-loss implications.

These results are strictly confined to an analysis involving the mean-variance analysis of risk in the presence of a utility function that is quadratic or to which a quadratic form is an acceptable nonlinear approximation. However, it turns out that when a less restrictive set of assumptions on utility and risk are adopted, the conclusions are reasonably robust in many circumstances.[9]

It might be thought that this reflects the inherent bias involved in permitting the Exchequer to participate fully in any realized gain but to avoid or reduce exposure to a realized loss. Implicitly, full-loss offset, in which the Exchequer participates proportionately in gains and losses, might be expected to avoid this deadweight loss. This, however, is not the case. Counter-intuitively, perhaps, but nevertheless demonstrably, full-loss offset applied to the capital gains tax in the (normal) case of the risk-averse portfolio holder results unambiguously in a shift in the underlying chosen position on the risk-return trade-off as a consequence of increasing (from zero or any positive rate) the effective rate of taxation. That shift is towards a higher preferred level of risk. The intuition behind this is simple: with full-loss offset, an increase in the tax rate reduces risk and expected return *pari passu*. Risk aversion implies a diminishing marginal utility of income. At a lower expected income level, a risk-averse portfolio holder will choose to increase risk in order to replace lost income. Hence, under full-loss offset the chosen value for the portfolio's risk parameter will increase as the private wealth-holder adjusts to the tax. The Exchequer as sleeping partner has to accept this outcome: a higher expected value of the tax yield but increased variability.

The foregoing has interesting implications for the level and changes in the level of the effective rate when associated with changes in the approach to allowable deductions. First, starting at a low or zero tax rate, an initial *small* new tax or increase in the tax will increase the asset holder's preferred risk profile with zero or full-loss offset. However, with full-loss offset there is no substitution effect operating in favour of risk reduction. The substitution effect is negatively related to the degree of loss offset. It would seem to follow that, if the tax authorities wish to minimize the excess burden of the tax as measured by the consequent impact on portfolio composition, an initial *small* imposition of (or increase in) taxation should be accompanied by low to zero loss offset. To minimize the impact of a rate change on portfolio composition, a rise in the rate should be accompanied by a reduction in loss offset; a fall in the rate should be accompanied by an increase in loss offset.

With an existing *high* rate, these conclusions are reversed. Low offset at high rates results in reduced preferred levels of risk. Hence, if the rate is increased, portfolio composition neutrality requires improved loss offset. In tabular form, these conclusions can be presented as follows.

Existing Rate	*Low*	zero	High
Rate Change	+	-	+
Loss offset change	-	+	+

The definition of *high* and *low* rates is in terms of the impact of a rate change under zero offset. That is, a high rate is one at which the substitution effect of a rate change dominates the income effect while a low rate is one at which the income effect dominates the substitution rate. This has to be determined empirically.

In the Irish experience, it is interesting to note that although the applicable rate has moved between 60% and 20% over a 25-year period, no non-trivial change has ever been contemplated in the provisions governing loss offset. This is at least consistent with the general design of corporate and individual taxation over most of the period although this has been to some extent modified recently with the implementation of a schedular approach to establishing tax liability. Under this approach, each separate component element in gross income is separately assessed. Expenses or offsets are applied only to the relevant income element. A loss under one schedule is not taken into account in computing tax liability under others but is allowed only against income under that schedule in future years. If full-loss offset were to be introduced, it would involve allowing realized capital losses against taxable income from other sources in the same tax period. This was expressly rejected.

The conclusion has to be that the way in which the tax has been implemented has been based on a lack of knowledge or a lack of interest in the marginal impact on risk taking. In designing a regime, or in modifying it, surely such concerns ought to be a major element.

This has not been because the matter has been ignored. The system in Ireland has been more or less unchanged structurally since it was introduced in 1975 and modified in 1978. In 1982, the Commission on Taxation established in 1980 studied it. That Commission made several recommendations for reform of the structures in the context of a complete reform of direct taxation (The Commission on Taxation 1982: 201–20). Since the overall reforms it urged were not adopted, many of the specific amendments suggested for the capital gains tax became redundant. However, on the point of loss offset the Commission was unambiguous in calling for full-loss offset against other income as being the only intellectually respectable position that a taxing authority could adopt. It noted that the limitations on such offsets in the American code owed much to a desire to "protect the tax yield" arising from the impact of capital losses on federal income-tax yields during the Great Depression but argued that this stance is not logically sustainable.

Notes

1. A good source for the structure and details of the CGT as introduced is to be found in Bale 1977. For subsequent years and a general account of modifications to the tax, the interested reader should consult the annual review of the Irish tax code produced by the Institute of Taxation in Ireland, which contains for any year the law and practice as they stood and any modifications in that year's finance legislation. The current edition is Corry, McLaughlin and Martyn (no date). A detailed account of the law and practice affecting CGT is produced annually as well. The current (11th) edition is Appleby and Carr (no date).
2. Irish income tax law was based on the 1918 codification legislation of the Westminster parliament, which was inherited by the Government of the Irish Free State when that dominion came into being in December, 1922. The British schedular system applied income tax differentially to incomes derived by individuals under five general classifications, schedules A, B, C, D and E. Schedules A and B referred to incomes from real property in agriculture and non-agricultural holdings, largely on the basis of notional rates. Schedule C covered, *inter alia*, income from the rental of property. Schedule D referred to the profits (income) from a trade, profession or avocation (in effect non-employee income). Schedule E referred to income from employment. If an accrual to an individual did not fall into one or other of these categories it was not an income for taxation purposes.
3. In Ireland about 80% of households own their homes, an extremely high percentage by European standards. Home ownership is the largest single category of privately held wealth.
4. The structure of exemptions for CGT in Ireland has always been based on an annual amount. It has varied as between an amount per individual or per household but is not subject to any life-time limit. This feature of the regime is consistent with the basis for the tax as a complementary income tax rather than as a form of capital taxation. For CAT (which includes transfers *inter vivos* as well as on death) life-time limits do apply.
5. At present, corporation tax is being reduced in stages towards a target of 12.5% for all corporations by 2003. The current 10% rate ap-

plying to manufacturing sector profits will be raised to 12.5% after 2011 and other concessionary 10% rates will be raised to 12.5% from 2006.
6 This does not apply to own account trading, where different rules apply.
7 The material in the next few paragraphs is an exposition of the results of standard neo-classical analysis of the tax-payer's response to the imposition of capital gains tax with imperfect or full-loss offset. A full exposition of the results of this analysis may be found in Musgrave 1959: chap. 14.
8 I assume a conventionally well defined and well behaved utility function defined over risk and yield and a monotonic risk-yield trade-off.
9 Using Arrow's definitions of absolute and relative risk aversion, $A(W) = -(UO(W)/UN(W))$ and $R(W) = -W(UO(W)/UN(W))$, respectively, Stiglitz has shown that, in the presence of full-loss offset, a general expected-utility-of-wealth function implies that private risk-taking will increase if the following conditions hold true: (1) the yield on the non-risky asset is zero; and $AN(W) > 0$ or $AN(W) < 0$ and $RN(W) > 0$ (Arrow's conjecture); (2) the yield on the non-risky asset exceeds zero and $AN(W) > 0$ and $RN(W) > 0$. A general expected-utility-of-wealth function does allow risk-taking to be reduced by taxation with full-loss offset if these conditions are not met. See Stiglitz 1969: 263–83.

References

Appleby, T., and F. Carr (no date). *The Taxation of Capital Gain.*

Bale, N. (1977). *Capital Taxation—Finance Act 1977 Edition.* Dublin: The Institute of Taxation in Ireland.

Capital Taxation (1974). Prl. 3688. Dublin: The Stationery Office.

Corry, T., J. McLaughlin, and J. Martyn (no date). *Taxation Summary, Republic of Ireland.*

Musgrave, R.A. (1959). *The Theory of Public Finance.* New York: McGraw Hill.

National Economic and Social Council (NESC) (1974). *Comments on Capital Taxation Proposals* (prl.3943). Dublin: The Stationery Office.

Sandford, C.T. (1988). *Taxation of Net Wealth, Capital Transfers and Capital Gains of Individuals.* Paris: OECD.

Stiglitz, J. (1969). The Effects of Income, Wealth and Capital Gains Taxation on Risk Taking. *Quarterly Journal of Economics* 83: 263–83.

The Commission on Taxation (1982). *First Report: Direct Taxation.* Dublin: The Stationery Office.